VICTORIOUS!
Defeating Bullies and Giants God's Way

See how God handles giants, bully bosses, school yard bullies, bully coworkers, mean girls, family bullies, and especially wicked bullies.

Darnnell Reese

Copyright © 2017,2025 Darnnell Reese
First published 2017, Second Edition 2025
Published by Victorious With God, Fort Washington, MD
Amazon Author Central: Darnnell D Reese
IG: darnnells
YouTube: Darnnell Reese
https://reeseauthor.com
darnnells@gmail.com
All rights reserved.

ISBN-9798993853642

DEDICATION

This book is dedicated to my husband and best friend Terrence who is always a blessing to me. Thanks for your unselfish love and support in this journey and for always humbly representing Christ in all your ways. I truly cherish and appreciate you for everything. You are a rare and precious gift.

Table of Contents

ACKNOWLEDGMENTS

Thank you Deidra for your encouragement of me to write this book. For also listening to me and giving me honest and critical feedback and insight. You are a wonderful daughter and best friend. You have a heart for God by always being honest and striving for excellency in your walk with Him. Thank you for believing that this was something that had to be written to help others who were in despair and did not know the Way out.

Chapter 1

Can plunder be retrieved from a giant, prisoners of war gotten back from a tyrant? But God says, 'Even if a giant grips the plunder and a tyrant holds my people prisoner, I'm the one who's on your side, defending your cause, rescuing your children. And your enemies, crazed and desperate, will turn on themselves, killing each other in a frenzy of self-destruction. Then everyone will know that I, God, have saved you--I, the Mighty One of Jacob.'

Isaiah 49:24-26, MSG

Big bullies generally come in all shapes, sizes, and forms. They can be an irascible, hot-tempered person in the mall parking lot, a fellow customer waiting in line at the DMV, or the person sitting behind you at the movie theater, who is quick to pick a fight with a perceived weaker person. Or, it can be in the form of a bureaucratic bully like the Internal Revenue Service conducting an audit on your financials for the last five years. Or, it can be an unexpected illness or situation that causes a sudden onset of overwhelming stress due to the magnitude and severity of the crisis. Any of these situations can look and feel so gigantic and impossible to overcome when you look at them from an impotent mindset that most humans naturally have.

The Bible contains plenty of these big bully situations that wreaked havoc on the lives of humans and the Bible clearly showed what God did to rid these oppressors from the lives of His people. The key to fighting any type of bully is to allow God to fight your battles for you. Most bullies, and/or turbulent life events are large and intimidating. But not to God. So partnering with God is your best defense against life's bullies.

Goliaths and Other Big Bullies

Remember the story of David and Goliath (guh-LYE-uth)? Well, Goliath was a descendant of a race of giants known as the Nephilim (NEFF-ih-lim). The giants or Nephilim were blood-thirsty, gluttonous, part-man, part fallen angel hybrids. "The Nephilim were on the earth in those days --- and also afterward--- when the sons of God went to the daughters of humans and had children by them. They were the heroes of old, men of renown" (Genesis 6:4, NIV). This underwhelming Bible passage never really caught my attention until I started to really study the Bible. When I fully comprehended this revelation, I was utterly astonished. Literal giants walked the earth!?! I started to research this fascinating topic and other mind-blowing biblical expositions that were never talked about in church. Jude 1:6-7 (NIV) further expounds on the fallen angels referenced in Genesis 6:4; "...And the angels who did not keep their position of authority but abandoned their proper dwelling---these He has kept in darkness bound with everlasting chains for judgment. In a similar way, Sodom and Gomorrah and the surrounding towns gave themselves up to sexual immorality and perversion. They serve as an example of those who suffer the punishment of eternal fire." Simply put, Jude is explaining that these fallen angels, lusting after the daughters of man, willingly and knowingly engaged in sexual relations and the Nephilim was the progeny of those relations. The Nephilim were truly freaks of nature and what the Lord considered abominations.

What sparked God's wrath against them? Genesis 6:1-3 (NIV) states, "When human beings began to increase in number on the earth and daughters were born to them, the sons of God saw that the daughters of humans were beautiful, and they married any of them they chose. Then the Lord said, 'My Spirit will not contend with humans forever, for they are mortal; their days will be a hundred and twenty years.'" Genesis 6:5-9 (AMP) goes on to say, "The Lord saw that the wickedness (depravity) of man was great on the earth, and that every imagination or intent of the thoughts of his heart were only evil continually. The Lord regretted that He made mankind on the earth, and He was [deeply] grieved in His heart. So the Lord said, 'I will destroy (annihilate) mankind whom I have created from the surface of the earth --not only man, but the animals and the crawling things and the birds of the air--because it [deeply] grieves Me [to see mankind's sin] and I regret that I have made them.' But Noah found favor and grace in the eyes of the Lord. Noah was a righteous man [one who was just and had right standing with God], blameless in his [evil] generation; Noah walked (lived) [in habitual fellowship] with God."

Noah had to have faced horrendous and ongoing threats living among all the wickedness that surrounded him. He and his family may have been constantly tormented and victimized by the giant bullies living and existing on the earth. Because Noah was God's friend and faithfully walked with God, I'm certain that Noah cried out to God about the fear he felt or the injustices he may have suffered at the hands of wicked humans. Because God is always a defender of His children, He protected Noah at all times. Because God cared so much for Noah, Genesis 6:11-12, AMP further states, "The [population of the earth] was corrupt [absolutely depraved--spiritually and morally putrid] in God's sight, and the land was filled with violence [desecration, infringement, outrage, assault, and lust for power]. God looked on the earth and saw how debased and degenerate it was, for all humanity had corrupted their way on the earth and lost their true direction." God is our Heavenly Father and He will protect us.

Because of these things, God said to Noah, "I am going to put an end to all people, for the earth is filled with violence because of them. I am surely going to destroy both them and the earth. So make yourself an ark of cypress wood; make rooms in it and coat it with pitch inside and out" (Genesis 6:13-14, NIV). This epic event was called the Great Flood. God will literally destroy mankind and save His children in the process to protect His children from evil and wickedness. He does not want His flock to suffer, especially those who walk with Him and who trust, rely, and lean on Him. God's plan was to protect the people who had not corrupted themselves, and that was found amongst Noah and his immediate family: his wife, his three sons: Japheth (JAY-feth), Shem, and Ham and their wives, their livestock and other undefiled animals and birds.

Then God sealed them all in this anointed ark and opened the floodgates of heaven. According to Genesis 6:17-18 (AMP) "The flood [the great downpour of rain] lasted 40 days and 40 nights on the earth; and the waters increased and lifted up the ark and it floated high above the land. The waters became mighty and increased greatly on the earth and the ark floated on the surface of the waters." "...All living beings that moved on the earth perished" (Genesis 7:21, AMP). "...God destroyed (blotted out, wiped away) every living thing that was on the surface of the earth; man and animals and the crawling things and the birds of the heavens were destroyed from the land. Only Noah and those who were with him in the ark remained alive. The waters covered [all of] the earth for a hundred and fifty days (five months)" (Genesis 7:23-24, AMP), to thoroughly cleanse the earth of those corrupt and wicked humans, animals and Nephilim.

Trust and believe that God will deliver you from your enemies. It may not be as global a scale as the Great Flood, but for those who put their trust in the Lord, He will fight your battles with shock and awe! "Do not be

afraid, for I am your God. I will strengthen you, be
assured I will help you; I will certainly take hold of you
with my righteous right hand [a hand of justice, of
power, of victory, of salvation]" (Isaiah 41:10, AMP).

God will continue to fight giants for you because He
knows that evil persists and is never a one and done
happening. After fighting one giant circumstance,
another one will creep up and try to overtake you.
Deuteronomy 2:20-21 (NIV) speaks about postdiluvian
giants (giants who came after the flood) who in the
same fashion (evil, corrupt, perverse, and wicked) as
the antediluvian (pre flood) giants, were causing
trouble for God's people yet again: "That too was
considered a land of Rephaites (REFF-ay-ites), who used
to live there; but Ammonites ((Ammon-ites)
descendants of Lot) called them Zamzummites (zam-
ZUM-mites). They were a people strong and numerous
and as tall as the Anakites (ANN-uh-kites). The Lord
destroyed them from before the Ammonites who drove
them out and settled in their place." You may be
wondering, 'Why does God allow evil people to persist
and why does this keep happening to me?' Those are
not the right questions. God works through humans,
and His power is manifested in our weakness.

The Bible states in 1 Corinthians 1:27 (AMP) "But God
has selected [for His purpose] the foolish things of the
world to shame the wise [revealing their ignorance],
and God has selected [for His purpose] the weak things
of the world to shame the things which are strong

[revealing their frailty]." And, 2 Corinthian 12:9 (AMP) reiterates that God works through man's weakness; "My grace is sufficient for you, for my power is made perfect in weakness." God loves you and this is something you must understand.

You have giants in your life, not so you can feel powerless, but so that you can TRIUMPH *and* to be POWERFUL *in* GOD! This is what glorifies God.

It's like a good volleyball game; the ball is strategically set up for the "hitter" to spike the ball. Although, this is a very simplistic analogy, the point is, God needs only for us to move the ball into position (work with Him through obedience and prayer) and He will swiftly and violently smash the ball down to the ground. That's what God does to bullies and giants every day. Even if you have to lock yourself in a room and repeat over and over, "God loves me", do it! Defeating giants or any other bully in your life requires you to have the proper mindset regarding God's love toward you. Here is what God told Jeremiah when he became weary and depressed after fighting evil: "So, Jeremiah, if you're worn out in this footrace with men, what makes you think you can race against horses? And if you can't keep your wits during times of calm, what's going to happen when troubles break loose like the Jordan in flood? Those closest to you, your own brothers and cousins, are working against you" (Jeremiah 12:5, MSG).

Anyone who has ever been tormented by a big bully will find comfort, strength, and encouragement in God's word. They will also find out how to properly defend, fight, and protect themselves from them. The answer is to take all of your giants to God. Tell Him in whatever way you like; out loud, under your breath, in writing, in silent prayer, in song, in poems. It matters not to God, just reach out and tell Him. Genesis 4:10 (AMP) tells how Abel's blood cried out to God from the ground because his brother Cain murdered him: "The Lord said, 'What have you done? The voice of your brother's [innocent] blood is crying out to Me from the ground [for justice].'" God will hear you when you cry out to Him. And in Genesis 18:20-21 (MSG) it states "...The cries of the victims in Sodom and Gomorrah are deafening; the sin of those cities is immense. I'm going down to see for myself, see if what they're doing is as bad as it sounds. Then I'll know." God fights for all of His people! In Exodus 22:22-24 (AMP) God said, "You shall not harm or oppress any widow or fatherless child. If you harm or oppress them in any way, and they cry at all to Me [for help], I will most certainly hear their cry and My wrath shall be kindled and burn; I will kill you with the sword, and your wives shall become widows and your children fatherless." God takes our cries very seriously! Jesus also confirms our cries are heard in Luke 18:7-8 (NIV); "And will not God bring about Justice for His chosen ones, who cry out to Him day and night? Will He keep putting them off? I tell you, He will see that they get justice, and quickly. However, when the Son of Man comes, will He find faith on the earth?" All of these passages should be inculcated in your heart and mind just how much God loves you and will beat a bully to dust and ashes for His children. Just like He orchestrated the Great Flood to rid the earth of giants, He also rids the earth of people who behave as bully giants.

As history has a way of repeating, unfortunately, more giants came after the Great Flood. Again, God saw and heard of their wickedness, depravity, and injustice they inflicted on His people. In Genesis 15:18-21 (NIV) God told Abraham, "To your descendants I give this land, from the Wadi of Egypt to the great river Euphrates, the land of the Kenites (KEE-nites), Kenizzites, Kadmonites (KAD-muh-nites), Hittites (HIT-tites), Perizittes (PAIR-ih-zites) Rephaites (REFF-ay-ites), Amorites (AM-uh-rites), Canaanites (KAY-nun-ites), Girgashites (GUR-guh-shites) and Jebusites (JEB-yoo-sites)." If you haven't already guessed, all these "ites" were giants and God was preparing to slay every last one of them! God had explained to Abraham in a prior passage exactly when he would begin disposing of those giants and give the land to Abraham's descendants; "In the fourth generation your descendants will come back here, for the sin of the Amorites has not yet reached its full measure" (Genesis 15:16, NIV). This simply meant that their evil had not reached its absolute worst. God allows people to correct their behavior, but these giant bullies were incorrigible and deserved to be annihilated. If nothing was done to exterminate them, God's children would not be able to survive on earth.

Bullies don't stop on their own. That is why God is concerned with our human condition and is extremely serious about defending us from the potential and actual evil of bullies. He will not stand idly by while we get treated like lambs led to the slaughter. Never doubt what God can do to help you. "God is our refuge and strength, a very present help in trouble. Therefore will not we fear, though the earth be removed, and though the mountains be carried into the midst of the sea" (Psalm 46:1-2, KJV).

Even when you are quaking and shaking violently out of fear, God will give you the victory. Achieving total victory does require you to trust in Him, believe in Him, and rely on Him. Trusting is allowing God to defend you and not trying to defend or fight in your own power. This does not mean to stand still and let a bully harm you in any way. It plainly means; do not devise any scheme or plan of revenge of your own concoction. Believing in Him means that you understand and know that He is here to help you and to protect you and that He will. To rely on Him means to take your cares, worries, fears, cries, pains, and suffering to Him. He will comfort you and also give you the grace to get past your suffering. Doing these simple actions activates God's awesome power and allows His ineffable and unimaginable power to be released in your life. God's awesome power is exponentially more powerful than the highest tsunami waves or any category 5 hurricane, and way beyond comprehension. Trying to even fathom it does not compute. Look at the news and see devastation and destruction anywhere in the world due to natural disasters; the intensity of the destruction exceedingly lacks in comparison to what God's power is like. It's utterly terrifying in magnitude and scope. God created the universe out of nothing! The "Big Bang" theory of how the universe was created, even in its awesomeness is an understatement. What God does is cataclysmic, astronomical, and earth shattering. It's something that no human would like to see, but ultimately one day, we will all see.

Even when you are scared and shaking violently out of fear, try not to speak doubt and fear when asking God for your victory. God will give you the victory, but speaking doubt and fear can stall or delay your victories. When you are hurting, scared, suffering and being victimized, you surely don't want to have any unnecessary delays for relief. Speaking negatively or accepting defeat before even trying can remove God's anointing on our life. Why would you need His anointing, if you are already conceding the victory? In Numbers 13:27-29 (MSG), some of the Israelite scouts brought back a negative report to the rest of the Israelite camp based on their fear and doubt:

We went to the land you sent us and Oh! It does flow with milk and honey! Just look at this fruit! The only thing is that the people who live there are fierce, their cities are huge and well-fortified, worse yet, we saw descendants of the giant Anak. Amalekites (uh-MAL-uh-kites) are spread out in the Negev; Hittites, Jebusites, and Amorites hold the hill country; and the Canaanites are established on the Mediterranean Sea and along the Jordan. Caleb interrupted, called for silence before Moses and said, 'Let's go up and take the land--now. We can do it.' But the others said, 'We can't attack those people; they're way stronger than we are.' They spread scary rumors among the People of Israel....We scouted out the land from one end to the other---It's a land that swallows people whole. Everybody we saw was huge. Why, we even saw the Nephilim giant (the Anak giants come from the Nephilim). Alongside them we felt like grasshoppers. And they looked down on us as if we were grasshoppers.

This is a prime example of why people will not have victory over problems, issues, troubles, illnesses and other giants in their life. Stop speaking defeat when you are afraid. If others around you are speaking fear and doubt, separate yourself if they persist and do not stop their squawking. Fear is often an irrational emotion that manifests because something is unknown, and rather than drawing a logical conclusion, the mind jumps to the extreme opposite which allows for panic and wild emotional upheaval. Fear also can cause our brains to paralyze us by short-circuiting our muscular response during a crisis. Just like the Myotonic or fainting goats that fall over paralyzed when they are afraid. It's a similar response in humans. Humans then make things worse by speaking on the fear which paralyzes not only ourselves, but also those within earshot of our fear-mongering.

The Israelite's overreaction to what they saw caused God to remove His grace and anointing of helping them defeat those giants. There is no doubt in my mind that God would have handed every giant living in the land over to them in total defeat and annihilation. But because the bad report had such an enervating effect on all who heard, God had to scrap his plan for another 40 years just to be certain that all of the naysayers were no longer alive:

Except for Caleb the son of Jephunneh and Joshua the son of Nun, not one of you shall enter the land in which I swore [an oath] to settle you. ~But your children whom you said would become plunder, I will bring in, and they will know the land which you have despised and rejected. ~But as for you, your dead bodies will fall in this wilderness. ~'Your sons shall be wanderers and shepherds in the wilderness for forty years, and they will suffer for your unfaithfulness (spiritual infidelity), until your corpses are consumed in the wilderness. ~According to the number of days in which you spied out the land [of Canaan], forty days, for each day, you shall bear and suffer a year for your sins and guilt, for forty years, and you shall know My displeasure [the revoking of My promise and My estrangement because of your sin]....As for the men whom Moses sent to spy out the land, and who returned and made all the congregation murmur and complain against him by bringing back a bad report concerning the land, even those [ten] men who brought back the very bad report of the land died by plague before the Lord (Numbers 14:30-34,36).

Do yourself a great favor and get into agreement with God. If you are afraid, so be it. Just keep your mouth shut while being afraid. Remember that in Luke 1:19-20, the angel Gabriel, the sentinel of God, supernaturally silenced Zachariah's mouth throughout his wife Elizabeth's entire pregnancy with their son, John the Baptizer. This was done because Zachariah spoke unbelief and doubt that his wife would become pregnant since they both were very old. Fear is not shameful; It is the unbelief, or paralyzing inaction to fear which hinders our efforts at achieving total victory over life's big bullies and giants. It is exactly at these critical times that the best action is to be quiet, be still (free from disturbance, agitation or commotion), take your problems to God and wait patiently as He makes straight your path. To be still doesn't mean to stay in harm's way, it simply means to move forward in the face of fear while trusting God to do all that you are not able to do in your own power and strength. He will do it. Do not negate God's power with talk of defeat and negativity. He will deliver you. Just give Him the reins and step back. That's what trusting, relying and leaning on God means in the simplest terms. Let go and let God.

To those that habitually victimize their fellow man by behaving as big bullies and giants, please know that God has a special message for you regarding his flock: "As for you, my flock, this is what the Sovereign Lord says: I will judge between one sheep and another and between rams and goats. Is it not enough for you to feed on the good pasture? Must you also trample the rest of your pasture with your feet? Is it not enough for you to drink clear water? Must you also muddy the rest with your feet? Must my flock feed on what you have trampled and drink what you have muddied with your feet? Therefore, this is what the Sovereign Lord says to them: See, I Myself will judge between the fat sheep and the lean sheep. Because you shove with flank and shoulder, butting all the weak sheep with your horns until you have driven them away. I will save my flock and they will no longer be plundered. I will judge between one sheep and another" (Ezekiel 34:17-22, NIV).

TESTIMONY

On my 41st birthday in December 2012, my mother called to tell me she had just been diagnosed with cancer. She had been bleeding for months even though she had already entered menopause. Along with the heavy menstrual bleeding, she suffered from sporadic lower back spasm which left her vulnerable to falling due to debilitating weakness in her lower back and legs. We knew from the symptoms that all was not well. It was finally confirmed on my birthday. Although you never know exactly how to handle news like this, I knew that panic and wailing would not help the situation. My walk with God was not at all what it is now. I was always one to pray, but I had not begun to read, much less, study the word. I was a baby Christian in many ways. My immediate action was to get on my knees and pray. I prayed for grace to deal with this, healing for my mom and wisdom to do all that the crisis required. That's all I could do, because I didn't know anything else and my brain was not able to do much thinking. When I say my prayer was basic and elementary, I mean exactly that. I had no plan, thoughts, ideas, concepts. I was blank but I knew I needed God. My mom was numb as well. She didn't cry or react. She did all that was asked of her. She didn't resist, or fight us in any area. The cancer diagnosis scared her to the point of numbness. We took her for her follow-up oncology appointment where the doctor explained what stage she was, and what the recommended treatment was. While at the hospital, I observed that this hospital's workers lacked basic concern and care for their patients. I saw elderly patients walking without help and without any employees (orderlies, nurses, doctors) assisting or providing wheel chairs. I felt that God was imparting wisdom to me that I needed to take my mother to a hospital that actually cares for its patients and also specializes in cancer treatment.

The first giant I faced was getting my mother's primary care physician to provide a referral so that mom could go to a top oncologist I found through an internet search of "highly rated oncologists" based on cancer type. This was a giant because the primary care physician was the same doctor who never examined my mother even though my mom repeatedly complained to her that she was bleeding heavily after going through menopause. This doctor never bothered to examine her or refer her to someone else. She dropped the ball. This was also proof to me that this hospital did not have great concern for their patients. God's instructions was for me to politely ask that doctor to provide me with a written referral on hospital letterhead with all necessary signatures and contact information, in triplet, so that we would have one copy for her file, one to provide to the new physician and one just in case. God had me and my aunt, who is a longtime nurse, patiently and visibly wait outside of the doctor's office door until she did it, which took about two hours. Once she provided it, we graciously thanked her and never saw her face again. One giant was down a few more to go!

The second giant was switching my mother's insurance. At mom's next appointment, the new oncologist informed us, that although she currently honored my mother's insurance, at the beginning of the new year 2013, they would no longer accept that insurance. Everyone knows the bureaucracy involved with changing insurance carriers after open enrollment is never easy. Again, I prayed for God's grace to help me with this. He did it. I made a few calls to the number provided on the back of mom's Medicaid card and they gave me the contact information for the right department to make the switch to the new insurance. The switch was a covered event based on a life threatening illness and was done immediately. Hallelujah!!!! Second giant down!

The third giant was getting mom to stop smoking. She had been a smoker since her late teens when smoking was considered "cool". Although, she had tried to quit many times before, she couldn't. This was a huge giant because the new oncologist told my mother in no uncertain terms, she would not perform the surgery if she was still smoking by the time of the operation. My mom said she would definitely try.

As we were waiting to check out of the doctor's office, while we were in the waiting room, a breast cancer patient came in for her post-operative follow-up appointment. She was smiling and jubilant and happy to share her story of triumph over cancer with the help of this doctor. For whatever reason, she came over to my mom and told my mom how she almost died after her surgery because she did not heed the doctor's orders to not smoke. Apparently, she smoked after the surgery and had major complications, as well as surgical scar puckering, which is a deformity, resulting directly from smoking cigarettes after surgery. Mom's eyes were as wide as saucers. She began to pray and ask God to deliver her from smoking and HE DID!!! By the date of her surgery on February 27, 2013 mom had totally overcome her addiction to cigarettes. To this day, she has not smoked another cigarette, had zero complications from the surgery and the doctor totally and completely removed all the cancerous tumors in a radical hysterectomy. My mom completed several weeks of chemotherapy and targeted radiation. She never lost any hair nor had any skin bruising as a result. It felt as if God held our hands and took us high *and* above all of these problems with a divine ease and grace. God did all the work, opened every door, removed every mountain and slayed every giant.

The fourth and final giant was a personal one for me that was occurring contemporaneously to mom's cancer battle. In the last part of 2012, I applied for a new position within the agency that I work for, but a different division. A co-worker, who by the way was a former enemy turned "footstool", called and informed me that a new position was just announced and that I should apply. He said this division was a much better group and they offered regular tele-work schedules. Our group was not allowed to tele-work because of our manager's biases. All the more reason to apply. So, I heeded my co-worker's advice and applied. Just when mom was in the midst of her cancer battle and I was dutifully walking with her, the interview panels began. I thought it would be a one and done; a selection made and that would be it. That was not the case. I was asked to attend three interviews via remote video communication. Interviews are already nerve-wracking, but I was mentally incapable of preparing for these interviews because of all that was occurring with mom. Before each one, I prayed for God to help me speak intelligently and to say the right things. He must have done just that. After each interview I was utterly drained. I vividly remember prostrating myself on the floor in my home and telling God I could not take another interview.

I told him I am exhausted and have no idea where I stand. I was on autopilot at this point, and I was done! I asked God to get me off this emotional roller coaster. He did just that. On the day of mom's surgery, February 27, 2013, I left the hospital while my mom was in recovery. Before I left her, I laid hands on her sleeping body and prayed a prayer of complete healing and restoration over her. I left the hospital and headed home. Since I was already off, I looked forward to going home and watching mindless TV. I knew the "The King of Queens" would be on and I happily looked forward to it on the drive home. Once home, I lay in bed with my feet up and watched some Doug and Carrie. Just then, my cell phone rang and the caller I.D. had a 304 area code which is West Virginia. My agency's personnel office is in WVA, but I didn't put two and two together at that point. My mind was still not able to do much analytical processing; but God was in full control. The person on the other end of the phone, said, "Hi this is Laura with Bureau of Fiscal Services, is this Darnnell?", I said, "Yes." She said, "You applied for the position of xxx, are you still interested?" I said, "Yes!" She said, "GREAT!!!, because you were selected for the job!!!!" HALLELEUJA!! Fourth Giant down! God did all of this single-handedly and He did it swiftly and completely.

TESTIMONY

Soon after those giants, a really big giant tried to torment me and my husband in the form of the IRS. We received a letter from the IRS stating that we under reported our income for the prior tax year. The letter went on to explain that a 1099-MISC was received (from a company we were using as our property management for our rental property) which reported additional income we did not report. We had since dropped that company because of their unresponsive business practices and were with a new property management. The old company neglected to send us a 1099-MISC for the previous year, but sent one to the IRS. We tried to get all of our tax documents from them but to no avail. We had to estimate our income based on our monthly statements. We kept meticulous records and had access to the online portal. Subsequently, we found out that the old company attributed additional income to us that had actually been a refund to our tenants for their security deposit. This error caused our end of year totals to show more rental income to us, than was true. Once we discovered this was the cause of the error, we tried to explain it in writing and verbally to the IRS. The IRS being as difficult as they are, required *us* to get a corrected 1099 from the old property management company. That was where the battle of a lifetime began. This unresponsive company proved to be the most challenging struggle we had yet faced. We called and left voicemails, sent emails, called every employee on the dial-by-name, and each time we were ignored, transferred to no one, or passed to someone else who did not care. For the next three months we had to battle the IRS on one side of the table to get them to understand that it was not our mistake, meanwhile the IRS was telling us, until you have that company send us a corrected 1099, you will be on the hook for this additional monies. How UNFAIR is that?! We cried out loud and in silent, day after day, night after night in prayer and asked God to fight this battle for us. God did just that. He inspired me to contact the Better Business Bureau, the Attorney General for the state in which the old company resided (DC), and the State Attorney General for where the old company's new owner's resided (PA). God also had me email the new company's representatives and to formally submit a 3949-A form to report fraud and abuse of the tax system to the IRS regarding that old company. We suspected they fraudulently reported that 1099 because we dropped them as our property managers and they maliciously did this to cause us to have to pay thousands of dollars that we did not owe. I sent letters left and right; electronically and snail mail. And I got answers! Both state's attorney general offices took this matter very seriously and contacted the new owners of the former property management company. They obviously knew I would not relent until justice was served. No longer did that company pass me around like I was insignificant. They wrote up that letter so fast and provided me and the IRS with a corrected 1099. By the time it was all over, we received an apology letter from the new owners of the old company and a follow-up phone call from the Pennsylvania state attorney general office asking me if I was fully satisfied with the response from the old company's new owners. I certainly was and to GOD BE THE GLORY! I WILL CRY OUT TO GOD TO FIGHT ALL MY BATTLES, LARGE AND SMALL!

Chapter 2

Exploit or abuse your family, and end up with a fistful of air;
common sense tells you it's a stupid way to live
Proverbs 11:29, MSG

Familial Bullies are close kin that inflict pain and
suffering on those weaker than them who are in their
care or custody. "For out of the heart come evil
thoughts and plans, murders, adulteries, sexual
immorality, thefts, false testimonies, slanders (verbal
abuse, irreverent speech, blaspheming)" (Matthew
15:19, AMP). These relationships can be between
spouses, parents and children, children toward their
elderly parents, brothers and sisters, cousins, nieces and
nephews. Although family abuse, whether emotional,
physical, or sexual is common, it is not often mentioned
among Christians. The shame of it is too "embarrassing"
to admit. The stigma of abuse will cause people to
suffer in silence, rather than acknowledge that they
have an imperfect home. Our Lord and Savior Jesus
Christ boldly proclaimed that he did not come here to
bring peace: "Do you think I came to bring peace on
earth? No, I tell you, but division. From now on there will
be five in one family divided against each other, three
against two and two against three. They will be
divided, father against son and son against father,
mother against daughter and daughter against
mother, mother-in-law against daughter-in-law and
daughter-in-law against mother-in-law" (Luke 12:51-53,

NIV). In the last days, life or death choices are to be made by all men. Will you choose life or will you choose death? Jesus is the Truth, The Life and The Way. Choosing Jesus means putting aside every other thing and following Him. Some people in your family have already made a choice, either by deed or action, directly or indirectly to not follow the ways of Jesus. They may say they do or are, but you shall know them by their fruits (Matthew 7:16). "Not everyone who says to Me, 'Lord, Lord,' will enter the kingdom of heaven, but only he who does the will of My Father who is in heaven" (Matthew 7:21, AMP).

When people decide to not follow God's will, God will allow them to be overtaken by their own wicked devices, which oftentimes manifests as an evil or tormenting spirit. "Therefore they shall eat of the fruit of their own [wicked] way And be satiated with [the penalty of] their own devices" (Proverbs 1:31, AMP). Ongoing disobedience allows tormenting or evil spirits to overtake a person because the Holy Spirit is no longer dwelling within them. Those closest to the afflicted person are repeatedly abused or become the emotional target of the abusive person, who may or may not be aware that they are under the control of demonic and dark forces.

SAUL: Persecuting Commander in Chief of Young David

Before young David became king of Israel, King Saul, the first King of Israel, disobeyed God a few times too many and God regretted making him King. "Then the word of the LORD came to Samuel, saying, 'I regret that I made Saul king, for he has turned away from following Me and has not carried out My commands'" (1 Samuel 15:10-11, AMP). Saul was foolish and defiant in going on his own (wicked) way. Saul even tried to justify his disobedience by debating his case with Samuel and said, "I have obeyed the voice of the Lord, and have gone on the mission on which the LORD sent me, and have brought back Agag the king of Amalek, and have completely destroyed the Amalekites. But the people took some of the spoil, sheep and oxen, the best of the things [that were] to be totally destroyed, to sacrifice to the LORD your God at Gilgal." Samuel said, "Has the LORD as great a delight in burnt offerings and sacrifices As in obedience to the voice of the LORD? Behold, to obey is better than sacrifice and to heed [is better] than the fat of rams" (1 Samuel 15:20-22, AMP).

God immediately told Samuel His plans to select a new king. "As Samuel turned to go [away], Saul grabbed the hem of his robe [to stop him], and it tore. So Samuel said to him, 'The LORD has torn the kingdom of Israel from you today and has given it to your neighbor, who is better than you'" (1 Samuel 15:27-28, AMP).

When Samuel anointed David, son of Jesse the Bethlehemite, with the horn of oil in the presence of his brothers, the Spirit of the LORD came mightily upon David from that day forward (1 Samuel 16:13). And the LORD removed his spirit from Saul: "Now the Spirit of the LORD departed from Saul, and an evil spirit from the LORD tormented and terrified him. Saul's servants said to him, 'Behold, an evil spirit from God is tormenting you'" (1 Samuel 16:14-15, AMP). God withdrawing His Spirit from Saul in effect created a vacuum or void in Saul's soul and made Saul vulnerable for an evil spirit to come into him. Jesus warns in Matthew 12:43-45 (NIV), "When an impure spirit comes out of a person, it goes through arid places seeking rest and does not find it. Then it says, 'I will return to the house I left.' When it arrives, it finds the house unoccupied, swept clean and put in order. Then it goes and takes with it seven other spirits more wicked than itself, and they go in and live there. And the final condition of that person is worse than the first. That is how it will be with this wicked generation."

Saul chose, through his free will, to disobey God by not following and walking with God on several occasions. Although he was anointed king, he chose to go his own way, which deviated from God's instructions that were also given to him through God's prophet Samuel. By his actions, Saul made himself susceptible to evil and tormenting spirits which manifested as violent and abusive conduct toward young David who revered him like a father. Saul repeatedly tried to kill young David who was under Saul's authority as his subject but also as Saul's employee. Ironically, David was called to be Saul's personal musician to help sooth Saul when he was in the crisis of a demonic attack: "So Saul sent messengers to Jesse and said, 'Send me David your son, who is with the flock…then David came to Saul and attended to him…'" (1 Samuel 16:19,21, AMP).

Not only did Saul suffer from evil and tormenting spirits as a result of his disobedience, he apparently suffered from dementia. After summoning young David from his father's home, David becomes known as a brave and courageous warrior among Saul's army. However, Saul forgets and asks David who he was: "When David returned from killing [Goliath] the Philistine, Abner took him and brought him before Saul with the head of the Philistine in his hand. Saul asked him, 'Whose son are you young man?' And David answered, 'I am the son of your servant Jesse of Bethlehem'" (1 Samuel 17:57-58). Clearly Saul had already spoken to Jesse before when he initially asked if David could attend to him and play music for him. Now, Saul had forgotten all of this. His mind was becoming more and more troubled and he was becoming more and more irrational to the point where he completely turned on young David and began to try and kill him. "The next day an evil spirit from God came forcefully on Saul. He was prophesying in his house, while David was playing the lyre, as he usually did. Saul had a spear in his hand and he hurled it, saying to himself, 'I'll pin David to the wall.' But David eluded him twice. Saul was afraid of David, because the LORD was with David but had departed from Saul" (1 Samuel 18:10-12, NIV). Saul's disobedience opened the door for him to be attacked by several evil and tormenting spirits: dementia, psychosis, and jealousy.

Note how young David who is dutifully under Saul's

authority does not become insolent with Saul who is clearly not in his right mind. Even when he forgets who David is, David remains very reverent because it is always the godly thing to do. Also note that David did not just sit by and allow himself to be hurt by Saul. He protected himself by removing himself from Saul's presence. To elude means to escape or avoid, to escape from or avoid somebody or something by cunning, skill, or resourcefulness (Encarta ® World English Dictionary).

To be respectful to someone in authority or in a position of honor does not mean to become their victim. Honoring God should always dictate your actions, and that means using the good sense that God gave you to save yourself from harm.

Saul's final act of disobedience was when he consulted a medium in order to conjure up Samuel from the dead for advice. God had already set His face against mediums and spiritists in Leviticus 19:31 (AMP): "Do not turn to mediums [who pretend to consult the dead] or to spiritists [who have spirits of divination]; do not seek them out to be defiled by them. I am the LORD your God", and in Leviticus 20:6 (AMP) it says, "As for the person who turns to mediums [who consult the dead] or to spiritists, to play the prostitute after them, I shall set My face against that person and will cut him off from his people [excluding him from the atonement made for them]", and in Leviticus 20:27 (NIV): "A man or woman who is a medium or spiritists among you must be put to death. You are to stone them; their blood will be on their own heads." Saul knew better than to consult a medium, yet he knowingly disobeyed God and tried to disguise himself when he did this detestable thing:

> So Saul disguised himself, putting on other clothes, and at night he and two men went to the woman. 'Consult a spirit for me' he said 'and bring up for me the one I name' (1 Samuel 28:8, NIV). The medium realizes that it was the king who was before her and was scared to continue the séance. 'Surely you know what Saul has done. He has cut off the mediums and spiritists from the land. Why have you set a trap for my life to bring about my death?' Saul swore to her by the LORD, 'As surely as the Lord lives, you will not be punished for this.' Then the woman asked, 'Whom shall I bring up for you?' 'Bring up

Samuel', he said. When the woman saw Samuel, she cried out at the top of her voice and said to Saul, 'Why have you deceived me? You are Saul!' Samuel said to Saul, 'Why have you disturbed me by bringing me up?' 'I am in great distress,' Saul said. 'The Philistines are fighting against me, and God has departed from me. He no longer answers me, either by prophets or by dreams. So I have called on you to tell me what to do.' Samuel said, 'Why do you consult me, now that the LORD has departed from you and become your enemy? The LORD has done what he predicted through me. The LORD has torn the kingdom out of your hands and given it to one of your neighbors---to David. Because you did not obey the voice of the LORD and did not carry out His fierce wrath against the Amalekites, the LORD has done this thing to you today. The LORD will deliver both Israel and you into the hands of the Philistines, and tomorrow you and your sons will be with me'(1 Samuel 28:9-19, NIV).

Sure enough Saul and his sons were all dead the next day at that time.

And David remained humble and obedient and did not delight over the fact that Saul was killed. In fact, he sincerely mourned his death because he really cared for this man as a father figure and as God's anointed king. Also, David and Saul's son Jonathan were so close that they had a bond which was as close as two people could be. David not only lost his king, he lost his best friend. God saw David's heart and blessed him as a result. He became king of Israel just as God had already decided.

AMNON: Sexual Predator Who Abused His Own Sister

Unfortunately, not every situation of familial abuse happens to someone capable of escaping. Sometimes it happens to those least able to defend themselves; helpless women and children. How tragic when this happens, but God sees and knows all things, and the evil person will not escape God's wrath. "But whoever causes one of these little ones who believe and trust in Me to stumble [that is, to sin or lose faith], it would be better for him if a heavy millstone [one requiring a donkey's strength to turn it] were hung around his neck and he were thrown into the sea. If your hand causes you to stumble and sin, cut it off [that is, remove yourself from the source of temptation]! It is better for you to enter life crippled, than to have two hands and go into hell, into the unquenchable fire, where THEIR WORM DOES NOT DIE, AND THE FIRE IS NOT PUT OUT.]" (Mark 9:42-44, AMP). Someone who sexually violates a child is considered reprobate and reprehensible to our LORD and Savior Jesus Christ and He lets them know that if they are not able to control their unnatural proclivities they must remove themselves from the source of the temptation! That means, the adult has to do the right thing by dealing with their sexual deviance effectively and without hesitation. If allowed to fester, an innocent child will forever be affected by their selfish and perverted inclinations.

After Saul, David takes the throne and also takes many wives and concubines and has many children from those relationships. His only daughter, Tamar was an innocent virgin, still living in her parent's home with her older brother Absalom (AB-suh-lom) who was also a son of David. This is the awful account of what happened to Tamar as it is written in 2 Samuel 13:2-14, MSG:

Amnon (AM-non) was obsessed with his sister Tamar to the point of making himself sick over her. She was a virgin, so he couldn't see how he could get his hands on her. Amnon had a good friend, Jonadab (JON-uh-dab), the son of David's brother Shimeah. Jonadab was exceptionally streetwise. He said Amnon, 'Why are you moping around like this, day after day---you, the son of the king! Tell me what's eating at you.' 'In a word, Tamar,' said Amnon. 'My brother Absalom's sister. I'm in love with her.' 'Here's what you do,' said Jonadab. "Go to bed and pretend you're sick. When your father comes to visit you, say, 'Have my sister Tamar come and prepare some supper for me here where I can watch her and she can feed me.'" So Amnon took to his bed and acted sick. When the king came to visit, Amnon said, 'Would you do me a favor? Have my sister Tamar come and make some nourishing dumplings here where I can watch her and be fed by her.' David sent word to Tamar who was home at the time: 'Go to the house of your brother Amnon and prepare a meal for him.' So Tamar went to her brother

Amnon's house. She took dough, kneaded it, formed it into dumplings, and cooked them while he watched from his bed. But when she took the cooking pot and served him, he wouldn't eat. Amnon said, 'Clear everyone out of the house,' and they all cleared out. Then he said to Tamar, 'Bring the food into my bedroom, where we can eat in privacy.' She took the nourishing dumplings she had prepared and brought them to her brother Amnon in his bedroom. But when she got ready to feed him, he grabbed her and said, 'Come to bed with me, sister!' 'No, brother!' she said, 'Don't hurt me! This kind of thing isn't done in Israel! Don't do this terrible thing! Where could I ever show my face? And you---you'll be out on the street in disgrace. Oh, please! Speak to the king---he'll let you marry me.' But he wouldn't listen. Being much stronger than she, he raped her. No sooner had Amnon raped her than he hated her---an immense hatred. The hatred that he felt for her was greater than the love he'd had for her. 'Get up,' he said, 'and get out!'

Amnon was exhibiting all the signs of a tormented soul and of someone not in control of his emotions or his mind. He allowed himself to unnaturally and obscenely lust for his sister to the point of being sick and frustrated. He had an unclean and impure spirit ruling his actions, and making him want to violate his sister in the most wicked and heinous way because he was selfish and evil. He allowed himself to go down this wicked path because he refused to be obedient on many levels. Tamar even rebuked him, to no avail. Amnon was already a lost soul at that point and was beyond redemption. He had accepted the evil in his heart and was now embracing and relishing his evil actions. Tamar was clearly overpowered and could not escape her abuser. As a result of his actions, Tamar was deeply shamed and hurt to the point that she lived in her brother Absalom's home, a bitter and desolate woman. Once a beautiful, vivacious, virgin princess and now disgraced, discarded and undesired. Amnon not only took her virginity, but he also took her life as she once knew it and all the potential of what she was to be. Tamar lost her faith and never recovered from this selfish, hateful and brutal attack. I believe this is what Jesus meant when he said "But whoever causes one of these little ones who believe and trust in Me to stumble [that is, to sin or lose faith], it would be better for him if a heavy millstone [one requiring a donkey's strength to turn it] were hung around his neck and he were thrown into the sea. If your hand causes you to stumble and sin, cut it off [that is, remove yourself from the source of temptation]! It is better for you to enter life crippled, than to have two hands and go into hell, into the unquenchable fire, where THEIR WORM DOES NOT DIE, AND THE FIRE IS NOT PUT OUT.]

Amnon met an early and violent death as a result of his wicked abuse of his sister. Tamar's brother Absalom could not get over what happened to his sister and he became tormented with a spirit of revenge. Two years after raping Tamar, Absalom plotted and executed revenge on Amnon by killing him. Unfortunately, there were no winners in this family tragedy. David lost two sons and his only daughter was a bitter and desolate woman. The family was irreparably torn. Evil spirits only exist to torment person after person in every imaginable way; the spirit of sexual perversion in Amnon, the spirit of revenge in Absalom, and the spirit of unrelenting depression and anguish in Tamar. God is the antidote to evil and tormenting spirits.

NABAL: Debasing Husband and Rancorous Bully

Abigail was the beautiful and intelligent wife of a belligerent, cantankerous, hot-tempered man named Nabal (NAY-bal). Nabal was rich, but very harsh and evil in his dealings. "He had three thousand sheep and a thousand goats…" (1 Samuel 25:2, AMP). The terminology 'Evil in dealings' describes a person who most likely acquired wealth through ill-gotten gain. Someone who deals treacherously to obtain fortune is unscrupulous and does not have a heart for God. Having the heart of God will guide you to deal with everyone in an altruistic manner. Those who are evil, will put their needs, motives and desires ahead of others. Nabal was so harsh, his many household servants said he was a "worthless and wicked man that one cannot speak [reasonably] to him" (1 Samuel 25:17, AMP). Although Abigail was a patient, prudent and God-fearing wife, Nabal did not realize or appreciate it because he was a fool with a cold, greedy heart. In fact, his name meant fool. Nabal enjoyed his riches and material things above his wife or anyone for that matter. Because of his cruel behavior towards his wife as well other God-fearing people, Nabal stupidly and foolishly brought the wrath of God upon his own head. Colossians 3:19 (ESV) tells us "Husbands, love your wives, and do not be harsh with them", and, Proverbs 31:10 (ESV) says, "A wife of noble character who can find? She is worth far more than rubies." Nabal only saw value in his money and those things which would make him more money.

Before David began his reign as king, King Saul went insane and began trying to kill David. So David and his loyal army fled to the region where Nabal and Abigail lived. Already anointed by Samuel to be king, David was God's consecrated elect. To prepare young David for his calling, God allowed David to be persecuted by King Saul, as well as endure many harsh encounters along his escape routes; all designed to build David's faith and character while he learned to trust, rely, and lean on God to fight his battles. When David was bivouacking in the wilderness, he and his men protectively looked after the shepherds nearby tending their sheep. David and his men knew these particular shepherds belonged to Nabal, who they also knew was very well-off. So David instructed his men to go to where Nabal was celebrating "sheep-shearing festival" and ask him to be gracious to David and his men: "Go up to Nabal at Carmel and greet him in my name. Say to him: 'Long life to you! Good health to you and your household! And good health to all that is yours! Now I hear that it is sheep-shearing time. When your shepherds were with us, we did not mistreat them, and the whole time they were at Carmel nothing of theirs was missing. Ask your own servants and they will tell you. Therefore be favorable toward my men, since we come at a festive time. Please give your servants and your son David whatever you can find for them'" (1 Samuel 25:5-8, NIV). David could not have been more courteous! He was so sincere and respectful, it's hard to imagine anyone in his right mind refusing such a humble and gracious request.

But foolish Nabal could not go against his nature and was as mean as a snake toward David and his men. "Who is this David? Who is this son of Jesse? Many servants are breaking away from their masters these days. Why should I take my bread and water, and the meat I have slaughtered for my shearers, and give it to men coming from who knows where?" (1 Samuel 25:10-11, NIV). What a jerk! Nabal came up with every excuse to reject, devalue and humiliate David and his men. He accused them of being run-away slaves. It was clear that his men were soldiers. Secondly, the entire land knew of David and his many conquests and victories under King Saul. They actually had sayings in songs about David and his 10,000 and Saul and his thousands. David was hugely popular as the following two scriptures will attest; 1 Samuel 21:11, "But the servants of Achish said to him, 'Is this not David the king of the land?' Did they not sing of this one as they danced, saying, 'Saul has slain his thousands, And David his ten thousands?'" and again in 1 Samuel 29:5, "Is this not David, of whom they sing in the dances, saying, 'Saul has slain his thousands, And David his ten thousands?'" David was a legend and everyone knew it, but Nabal tried to pretend that David was a nobody and unworthy of Nabal's kindness, benevolence or humanity. God abhors inhospitable people. His word tells us in several scriptures how He feels about extending kindness to strangers: Ezekiel 16:49 (NIV),

"Now this was the sin of your sister Sodom: She and her daughters were arrogant, overfed and unconcerned; they did not help the poor and needy", Exodus 23:9, "You shall not oppress a stranger, since you yourselves know the feelings of a stranger, for you also were strangers in the land of Egypt", Leviticus 25:35, "Now in case a countryman of yours becomes poor and his means with regard to you falter, then you are to sustain him, like a stranger or a sojourner, that he may live with you" and Deuteronomy 27:19, "Cursed is he who distorts the justice due an alien, orphan, and widow And all the people shall say, 'Amen.'" God is very serious about caring for foreigners among you. Do not test him because He will vindicate the oppressed.

Nabal was so use to minimizing and subjugating his wife and his servants, he now had the arrogance to talk negatively and harshly to someone God anointed as the next king. Without a doubt this was definitely part of God's divine plan to put an end to Nabal and his wicked ways. In fact, God's word tells us, "The wicked will not prosper, for they do not fear God. Their days will never grow long like the evening shadows"

(Ecclesiastes 8:13, NLT). And because Nabal was such a fool, his own words brought him to ruin as we see in Proverbs 18:7 (NLT): "The mouths of fools are their undoing, and their lips are a snare to their very lives."

When David's men returned to tell him what Nabal said to him, he became blind with rage. He was nothing but kind and respectful to this man, but Nabal met his kindness with pure, unprovoked evil. David had had about enough of being mistreated by these bad-tempered elders whom he looked up to. First Saul, now Nabal. Saul was a king so David knew not to raise a hand against God's anointed, but Nabal was not anyone's anointed. He was now dead meat as far as David was concerned. He told his men "Strap on your swords!" and he and his four hundred men set out to bring Nabal down.

When Nabal's servants witnessed what their irascible boss said to David's men, they instantly knew that Nabal had just set in motion a cataclysm of events that did not bode well for Nabal nor the rest of Nabal's household. The servants immediately informed Abigail what her hot-tempered husband said and she "flew into action. She took two hundred loaves of bread, two skins of wine, five sheep dressed out and ready for cooking, a bushel of roasted grain, a hundred raisin cakes, and two hundred fig cakes, and she had it all loaded on some donkeys. Then she said to her young servants, 'Go ahead and pave the way for me. I'm right behind you.' But she said nothing to her husband Nabal" (1 Samuel 25:18-19, MSG). Abigail knew her husband was not approachable and did not take correction. Proverbs 23:9 (NIV) superlatively explains; "Do not speak to fools, for they will scorn your prudent words." Abigail had learned to judiciously manage her household affairs in the face of Nabal's nastiness and cruelty. As she was heading to take David and his men all those provisions, she actually met him on the same road as he was coming to take down Nabal. "David had just said, 'It's been useless---all my watching over this fellow's property in the wilderness so that nothing of his was missing. He has paid me back evil for good. May God deal with David, be it ever so severely, if by morning I leave alive one male of all who belong to him!'" (1 Samuel 25:21-22, NIV). Acting quickly, Abigail dismounts from her donkey and bowed down to David in humble submission and contritely apologizes for the way her husband had treated David and his men. Without excusing or condoning Nabal's wicked behavior she said, "Please pay no attention, my lord, to that wicked man Nabal. He is just like his name---his name means Fool, and folly goes with him. And as for me, your servant, I did not see the men my lord sent" (1 Samuel 25:25, NIV). Abigail was so wise to acknowledge Nabal's evil ways. Acknowledging Nabal's evil toward David was the right step in alleviating David's wrath. He was ready to kill Nabal, but because Abigail recognized that David had been wronged without cause, and was the victim of an evil bully fool; this helped to mollify David and quell his anger. Had it not been for Abigail's soothing apology for her husband's recklessness, David would have slain Nabal. Not only did Abigail calm David down, she prevented David from losing the anointing on his own life had he taken matters into his own hands regarding Nabal. Deuteronomy 32:35 (NIV) tells us "It is mine to avenge; I will repay. In due time their foot will slip; their day of disaster is near and their doom rushes upon them" and 1 Peter 3:9 (NIV) says, "Do not repay evil with evil or insult with insult. On the contrary, repay evil with blessing, because to this you were called so that you may inherit a blessing." Abigail expressed to David how God had surely anointed him and that he would soon be king, and for this reason he should not have the guilt of an avenged murder on his conscience. David was so appreciative of Abigail's thoughtfulness regarding his anointing, he blessed her and said, "Praise be to the LORD, the God of Israel, who has sent you today to meet me. May you be blessed for your good judgment and for keeping me from bloodshed this day and from avenging myself with my own hands" (1 Samuel 25:32, NIV). David also told her that had she not come so quickly to meet him, not one male belonging to Nabal would have been left alive by the next morning. He accepted Abigail's provisions and sent her home in peace.

When Abigail returned home to Nabal, he was drunk with wine and having a feast unto himself. He had no idea he had come within inches of being killed by David. Abigail chose not to inform Nabal while he was inebriated. But the next morning when he was sober, she told him all that happened after he insulted David and his men and sent them away with his harsh rebuke. As soon as she finished telling him everything that happened and all the disaster from which he narrowly escaped, Nabal's heart failed him and he became like a stone. Within ten days, Nabal was dead because the LORD struck him down.

"When David heard that Nabal was dead, he said, 'Praise be to the LORD, who has upheld my cause against Nabal for treating me with contempt. He has kept his servant from doing wrong and has brought Nabal's wrongdoing down on his own head'" (1 Samuel 25:39, NIV). And Abigail was blessed because of her faithfulness to God as well. David sent for her and asked her to be his wife. David wisely understood that Abigail was a rare find; priceless and worth far more than rubies.

Saul, Amnon and Nabal are three examples of familial bullies that were physically, sexually and emotionally abusive to those in their control. Abuse of any kind is wicked and God will punish those who commit these atrocities. Isaiah 3:11 (AMP) says "Woe to the wicked! Disaster is upon them! They will be paid back for what their hands have done" and neither Saul, nor Amnon, nor Nabal could escape God's just judgment. The best advice to all victims of evildoers is found in Psalm 37:7-11 (NIV): "Be still and wait patiently before the LORD. Do not fret when people succeed in their ways, when they carry out their wicked schemes. Refrain from anger and turn from wrath. Do not fret. It leads only to evil. For those who are evil will be destroyed, but those who hope in the LORD will inherit the land. A little while and the wicked will be no more. Though you look for them, they will not be found. But the meek will inherit the land and enjoy peace and prosperity."

TESTIMONY

My brother and I were raised by our single parent mom. I was two years older. We were both born when my mom was an unwed teenaged mother in the early 70's. Our father was very abusive to my mom and would beat, punch, slap, kick, knock her down for the slightest offense he felt she did to him. My father was also abused when he was a child by his dad and was also a product of a single parent mother with multiple children. My father's mother was an alcoholic. As a very young child I remember spending the night at his mom's apartment and the only thing in their refrigerator was a bottle of vodka. My dad's mother was nice, but as a young child I didn't really know her. I remember not being happy when I had to stay with her but it was not often. A few years after my brother was born in 1973, my mom and dad broke up for good. My mom now in her late teens / early twenties became bitter, abusive and hardened in general. She always had made it her mission to never allow anyone to get away with anything...not even her defenseless kids. She became our worst nightmare. As early as first and second grade we became targets of her unchecked rage. One particular memory was when she was fixing my hair one morning before school. I was very sensitive to pain when she would comb my hair, so I must have flinched or recoiled in pain as she was pulling and tugging on my hair. I remember whimpering and the next thing I knew she was whacking me upside my head with the back of the hair brush and then being pushed to the floor when she was done. I never knew what I had done but I remember never wanting to have my hair done again. I associated it with pain. My brother was abused far worse than me. Luckily, I was able to blend into the scenery like a potted plant to try and keep out of her way. Oblivious, my brother was a typical rambunctious boy and she attacked him whenever she became annoyed with him. When we were older about 10 and 12, my brother's primary chore was to take out the trash and clean the bathroom. Well, one night he forgot and was deep asleep when my mom came home from work. She woke him up out of his sleep with the lashing of the leather belt to his face and body, screaming profanities and awful names to him. I was in the bed across the small room and of course I woke up afraid, not knowing if I would be attacked as well for something I forgot. My brother was sent to take out the garbage that very night. We lived in an apartment, so the dumpster was outside on the back parking lot. Mom always justified her behavior by blaming us as being 'stupid', 'retarded', 'dumb-asses', 'oafs', or 'just like your daddy'. She also made jokes to her friends at our expense, in our presence. They would laugh, but I don't know if they were laughing out of embarrassment or if they were as heartless as she was. As a child, I believed it was the latter. But looking back, they probably did not know what to do or think. I wished that I could have been brave enough to help my brother, but I couldn't even help myself. At 17, I joined the army to get out of that home. I had made up my mind to never look back. Unfortunately, my brother ended up in the federal penitentiary to this very day. I believe he was also tormented and afflicted. The cycle was allowed to repeat. Consequently, he repeatedly got arrested in his teens for making poor choices. Like David, I eluded my mother! I also received God's love, healing and victory over my past, present and future. No longer a pitiful victim; I too am a giant killer. I have forgiven mom and have asked God to forgive her because I know she is very remorseful and did not know any better at the time.

Chapter 3

"Do not keep talking so proudly or let your mouth speak such arrogance, for the LORD is God who knows, and by him deeds are weighed."

1 Samuel 2:3 NIV

Mean girl bullies are one of the most offensive and unflattering of all types of women. They are so unkind and heartless in their treatment of people that they are an offense to all sense and sensibilities; sometimes appearing as beautiful and genteel creatures with impeccable mannerisms and charm, with beguiling sweetness and oozing with femininity, but beware! They are rotten inside and will corrode any who become unwittingly enamored with their sinister propensity.

Mean girls can be found almost everywhere a social structure exists; civic and community organizations, churches, schools, sororities, within families, the work place, and many other social organizations. Keeping an elevated status is the driving motivation of the mean girls. Mean girls fiercely and openly compete with anyone that may pose a threat to their position. Whether the person is even competing or is aware of the mean girl, matters not. The mean girl is aware of them and that is enough to get her primed for a hunt.

Some mean girls, but not all, travel in a pack, like

wolves. Like a wolf pack, mean girls are very social creatures and do many of their vicious activities in the company of the other mean girls. There is also a hierarchy and the dominant person is the 'alpha female'. The other members respect the authority of the alpha female and are inferior to her by choice and submission. The hunt of mean girls is the most deplorable, inhumane and degrading spectacle you would ever care to see. With hurtful, evil intent they poke fun at, humiliate, lie on, sneer at, jeer at, berate, lay traps for, insinuate, back-bite, and terrorize those they perceive as threats, employing character assassination to discredit, and ultimately eviscerate their target. If you ever witness such an outrageous act of barbarousness, do the right thing and call the bully out and protect the target by showing them kindness and gentleness. Whisk them away to safety from the bloodthirsty mean girls. Tell someone who can help and one who will make them go away. Tell God in prayer what you've seen and that you need His almighty hand right now! Do not enjoy the company of, or have friendly associations with a mean girl. She will turn her sights on you or anyone else in an instant. She can't beat everybody, so why not align yourself on the side of God. He can't stand a mean girl or any kind of bully.

PENINNAH: Jealous Insecure Mean Girl

Samuel, God's prophet in the Old Testament, had an intensely praying mother. (It is better than silver and gold to have a mother who persistently and boldly prays for her family!) Before Samuel was born, his mother Hannah's womb was closed and she could not get pregnant. Elkanah (el-KAY-nuh), her husband, loved Hannah dearly and was very sweet to her. Peninnah (peh-NIN-uh), Elkanah's other wife, had a brood of children; sons and daughters. "Whenever the day came for Elkanah to sacrifice, he would give portions of the meat to his wife Peninnah and to all her sons and daughters. But to Hannah he gave a double portion because he loved her, and the LORD had closed her womb" (1 Samuel 1:4-5, NIV). The hierarchy in Elkanah's household among his wives was not stated. But it is evinced through the scriptures from the time period, that Hannah was or was made to feel inferior to Peninnah because she could not bear children. Though Hannah was loved dearly, Jewish tradition placed extreme importance on bearing children. According to many Jewish people, procreation is considered a blessing from God and the first commandment given by God: "And you, be ye fruitful, and multiply; bring forth abundantly in the earth, and multiply therein" (Genesis 9:7, KJV).

Scriptures supporting this theory are found in Genesis where Jacob (grandson of Abraham, son of Isaac) also known as Israel, had two wives as well: Rachel and Leah. Rachel he loved, but Leah, not so much. God saw that Leah was not loved and God opened up her womb but Rachel was barren (Genesis 29:31, AMP). With each pregnancy Leah felt that her placement in her husband's eyes and their home, was more and more elevated: "Leah conceived and gave birth to a son and named him Reuben (See, a son!), for she said, 'Because the LORD has seen my humiliation and suffering; now my husband will love me [since I have given him a son]', Then she conceived again and gave birth to a son and said, 'Because the Lord heard that I am unloved, He has given me this son also.' So she named him Simeon (God hears). She conceived again and gave birth to a son and said, 'Now this time my husband will become attached to me [as a companion, for I have given him three sons.' Therefore he was named Levi" (Genesis 29:32-34, AMP). To emphasize the dynamics of how important having children are, Rachel's grief is sadly expressed in Genesis 30:1-3, "When Rachel saw that she conceived no children for Jacob, she envied her sister, and said to Jacob, 'Give me children, or else I will die.' Then Jacob became furious with Rachel, and he said, 'Am I in the place of God, who has denied you children?'" In an earlier point in biblical history an opposite dynamic erupted between Abram's (Abraham) wife and her handmaiden. In their scenario, Sarai (Sarah) knew who she was and did not allow Hagar to make her feel inferior. Once Hagar knew she was pregnant by Abram, she started to despise Sarai, incorrectly assuming the pecking order had changed in her favor. However, Sarai immediately subjugated Hagar, because she knew her position of authority as Abraham's only wife and did not need to compete with that woman. Eventually, Sarah conceived and had Isaac, the son born of the covenant between God and Abraham. Later on Sarah made Abraham send Hagar and her son Ishmael away from their home because Ishmael mocked Isaac. Sarah was well within her right as matriarch and wife to enforce her wishes to keep a peaceful home.

Peninnah obviously felt her position in the pecking order was at risk because despite Hannah being unable to conceive, Elkanah openly expressed his love and preference for Hannah. Peninnah was bitterly angry and jealous of Hannah even though she felt she was the one with all the power because she had the children. She tormented Hannah by poking at her about her inability to have children and making her feel less than a woman, or a failure to her husband, all with the intent to completely drive Hannah away permanently; either by death or by isolation and loneliness, employing mental cruelty as her weapon of choice. Peninnah was a mean girl. Since she bore Elkanah's children she probably thought that he should love *her* more than Hannah, and Hannah was nothing and had nothing with which to keep Elkanah loving her. The Bible confirms how Peninnah viciously and repeatedly tore Hannah down: "But her rival wife taunted her cruelly, rubbing it in and never letting her forget that God had not given her children. This went on year after year. Every time she went to the sanctuary of God she could expect to be taunted. Hannah was reduced to tears and had no appetite" (1 Samuel 1:6-7, MSG). One point not to be missed is the fact that Hannah had no appetite. Hannah could not even eat! Peninnah almost succeeded at her diabolical scheme to get rid of Hannah; her mental health was under constant attack and now her body was being starved. How could she survive under those conditions? Second point not to be missed is that Peninnah really became aroused to bitterness at the times when Hannah would go to the Sanctuary of God. Peninnah was the devil in disguise. The evil spirits within her were in fear of Hannah crying out to God. If Hannah had given up and let Peninnah torment her to isolation and silence, I believe Hannah would have died. In Matthew 26:38 (AMP) Jesus said, "My soul is deeply grieved, so that I am almost dying of sorrow." Then he went and prayed to His father in heaven. Hannah instinctively knew to keep praying and crying out to God at the sanctuary, in spite of her tormentor. Jesus gives that exact instruction to His disciples a few verses away in Matthew 26:41 (AMP): "Keep actively watching and praying that you may not come into temptation; the spirit is willing, but the body is weak."

Hannah's spirit reached out to God even though her body was weak and would have eventually failed. BUT GOD heard her crying, and He saved Hannah and healed her body in the process. He opened her womb and she became pregnant with Samuel. She did all that she had promised God and devoted Samuel to God as a Nazirite. Hannah had three sons and two daughters as a result of God hearing and answering her prayers. The Bible never mentions Peninnah ever again. My hopeful surmise is that Hannah's place as head wife was clearly and prominently defined and Peninnah was removed from (or relegated somewhere outside) the home so that Elkanah and Hannah lived in perpetual peace. GLORY HALLELUJAH! AND THANK GOD WE HAVE A FRIEND IN JESUS!!!!!

JEZEBEL: Sinister Queen of Mean Girl

Jezebel was another oppressively mean girl deserving of God's wrath and vengeance. She was written about in three books of the Bible; First and Second Kings in the Old Testament and the book of Revelation. In Revelation she is long dead, but because she was such a foul and rancid woman she was metaphorically mentioned. I'll share God's view of Jezebel as written in Revelation later, but for now, let's start with some of the vile and nasty things that Jezebel did to other people.

Jezebel, the princess daughter of Ethbaal (ETH-bay-al), King of the Sidonians, married king Ahab of Israel. The marriage was most likely a strategic alliance for both Israel and Sidonia as both nations were economic power players in the areas of trade and commerce. Ethbaal and his family were Baal (pronounced bail) worshippers. Baal was the primary god (a fertility god) of a pantheon of gods worshipped by the surrounding nations. Jezebel was loyal to her religious practices and king Ahab led Israel astray by following in her ways. When Ahab married Jezebel, he enthusiastically adopted Baal worship. He also erected Asherah (uh-SHEE-ruh) poles; a sacred tree or pole used to worship the goddess Asherah, another deity of those nations. When God first allowed the Israelites to enter the promised land of Canaan and helped them to dispossess the other nations, He specifically told His people through the prophet Moses, "Do not intermarry with them. Do not give your daughters to their sons or take their daughters for your sons, for they will turn your children away from following Me to serve other gods, and the LORD's anger will burn against you and will quickly destroy you. This is what you are to do to them: Break down their altars, smash their sacred stones, cut down their Asherah poles and burn their idols in the fire" (Deuteronomy 7:3-5, NIV). The Israelites were very forgetful to say the least and were a "stiff-necked" group of people. They continually went astray from God's instructions and did all that He told them not to do. When King Ahab disobediently married Jezebel he violated God's clear instructions. It is very important to God that you not yoke yourself to anyone or anything that will cause you to divide your loyalties away from Him. It's for your own well-being and benefit to obey God by not falling away because of your dangerous liaisons and alliances. Israelites were monotheistic and only followed the one true God. This marriage created a diametrically opposed conflict from the onset. You cannot serve God and Baal. God is a jealous God.

Because Ahab had married that detestable woman, he provoked God more than all the kings of Israel who were before him, and trust me when I say the other kings before him were progressively more awful than the preceding king. God immediately tried to get Israel to put aside their disobedience by sending them signs and warnings through His prophets. In 1 Kings 17:1 (MSG) God sent the prophet Elijah to warn Ahab, "As surely as God lives, the God of Israel before whom I stand in obedient service, the next years are going to see a total drought---not a drop of dew of rain unless I say otherwise." As soon as Elijah delivered His message to Ahab, He instructed Elijah to run to a distant place for his own protection, because God already knew what Jezebel was going to do next. She gathered all of God's prophets and killed them, for no other reason than to remove them so that the prophets of Baal would be the only revered and venerated prophets to the king and to the nations. Her quest for total power and domination was the reason she gave the order to kill all of God's prophets.

Jezebel was not only a mean girl, she was a complete

fool because only a brazen, foolhardy, idiot would fight against God Almighty. For three years, not a drop of rain fell on the land just as Elijah had prophesied. When God wanted to give Ahab the benefit of coming to his senses, He sent Elijah back to Ahab, even though Ahab and Jezebel were actively pursuing Elijah to kill him too. "When Ahab saw Elijah, Ahab said to him, 'Are you the one who is bringing disaster on Israel?' Elijah said, "I have not brought disaster on Israel, but you and your father's household have, by abandoning (rejecting) the commandments of the LORD and by following the Baals" (1 Kings18:17-18, AMP). Ultimately, Elijah proved to the unfaithful Israelites just how mighty and awesome their God was and killed over 450 Baal prophets in one day. God also brought back the rain.

When Jezebel heard that Elijah massacred her prophets, she was enraged to insanity. She sent a message to Elijah stating that she would kill him just as he had killed her prophets by that same time tomorrow. This really frightened Elijah, even though he had just killed 450 Baal prophets with the sword. Jezebel was so scary and diabolical, she put fear into his heart because he knew she was heartless, dangerous and of pure evil. Meanwhile, Elijah was sent out of Jezebel's reach, carrying out God's latest instructions. Because of Ahab and Jezebel's wicked ways, God declared final judgment against Ahab and the people of Israel who defiled themselves by worshipping Baal. The plans were set in motion. Undeterred in their wicked ways, Ahab and Jezebel conspired to bring ruin to their next-door neighbor, Naboth (NAY-both), who owned a vineyard adjacent to Ahab's property. Ahab wanted Naboth's vineyard for himself and made an offer to buy it. Naboth refused to sell it because it was a family owned property. Indignant over his rejection, Jezebel concocted a sinister plot to bring about Naboth's demise for not selling his vineyard to her husband. "She wrote letters over Ahab's signature, stamped them with his official seal, and sent them to the elders in Naboth's city and the civic leaders. She wrote 'Call for a fast day and put Naboth at the head table. Then seat a couple of stool pigeons across from him who, in front of everybody will say, 'You! You blasphemed God and the king!' Then they'll throw him out and stone him to death.' And they did it" (1Kings 21:8-11, MSG). "When Jezebel got word that Naboth had been stoned to death, she told Ahab, go for it, Ahab---take the vineyard of Naboth the Jezreelite for your own, the vineyard he refused to sell you. Naboth is no more; Naboth is dead" (1 kings 21:15, MSG). She was as cold as ice water and heartless as Satan himself.

God hears and sees all injustices especially excessively cruel and oppressive wickedness. He stepped in and spoke to Elijah and had him go to Ahab and let him know what would become of him as a result of this latest act of turpitude. When Elijah arrived he found Ahab already on Naboth's property claiming it as his own and Naboth was not even cold in the grave. Elijah prophesied to Ahab then and there and said, "God's word: What's going on here? First murder, then theft? God's verdict: The very spot where the dogs lapped up Naboth's blood, they'll lap up your blood---that's right, your blood" (1Kings 21:17-19, MSG). "As for Jezebel, God said, 'Dogs will fight over the flesh of Jezebel all over Jezreel...'" (1Kings 21:23, MSG).

Jezebel outlived her husband by 12 years. God is patient, but He is true to His word. Ahab's son Joram became king of Israel after his father was killed. Joram was killed by Jehu in Naboth's vineyard in the 12th year of his reign. Jehu was the son of Jehoshaphat son of Nimshi, (not the same Jehoshaphat king of Judah). God instructed Jehu to carry out His divine retribution on Ahab and Jezebel, their family and everyone in Israel who had followed the Baals. And Jehu carried out his orders with fervent zeal because he was obedient to the LORD. "When Jezebel heard that Jehu had arrived in Jezreel, she made herself up--- put on eyeshadow and arranged her hair--- and posed seductively at the window. When Jehu came through the city gate, she called down, 'So, how are things, 'Zimri,' you dashing king-killer?'" (2 Kings 9:30-31, MSG). Jezebel was the quintessential mean girl, attempting to charm and seduce with her feminine wiles, as if no one would see through her evil deception. She was delusional but Jehu did not fall for any of her conniving trickery. "Jehu looked up at the window and called, 'Is there anybody up there on my side?' Two or three palace eunuchs looked out. He ordered, 'Throw her down!' They threw her out the window. Her blood spattered the wall and the horses, and Jehu trampled her under his horse's hooves. Then Jehu went inside and ate his lunch. During lunch he gave orders, 'Take care of that damned woman; give her a decent burial---she is, after all a king's daughter.' They went out to bury her, but there was nothing left of her but skull, feet, and hands. They came back and told Jehu. He said, 'it's God's word, the word spoken by Elijah the Tishbite': In the field of Jezreel, dogs will eat Jezebel; The body of Jezebel will be like dog-droppings on the ground in Jezreel. Old friends and lovers will say, 'I wonder, is this Jezebel?'" (2 Kings 9:30-37, MSG). This last verse accurately and colorfully describes the digestive process of all animals. Once the dogs have eaten, they later produce waste, which is later evacuated from their system as manure. Jezebel's body is now manure. Jezebel was so disgusting to God, He took her wretched remains and ensured they would be treated in the manner worthy of her wicked life. When God is done with evil people, they are dung!

In the end, Jehu, son of Nimshi, put to death 70 of Ahab's sons by women other than Jezebel, killed Joram (son of Ahab), Ahaziah (son of Athaliah (ath-uh-LYE-uh)) and then killed Jezebel. Then Jehu killed 42 of Ahaziah relatives he happened to meet on the road as they were traveling to visit Ahaziah. And lastly, during a masterfully orchestrated, pretend "Baal worshiping ceremony", Jehu killed all the Baal prophets in a mass execution. Jehu's slayings wiped out the majority of Ahab's family, and by divine providence, the remaining evil family members massacred other family members in a God ordained turn of fate.

Our final analysis of this evil, mean girl, looks to the book of Revelation to further study on the abhorrent practices of Jezebel and her Baal worshiping idolatry: "But why do you let that Jezebel who calls herself a prophet mislead my dear servants into Cross-denying, self-indulgent religion? I gave her a chance to change her ways, but she has no intention of giving up a career in the god-business. I'm about to lay her low, along with her partners, as they play their sex-and-religion games. The bastard offspring of their idol-whoring I'll kill. Then every church will know that appearances don't impress me. I x-ray every motive and make sure you get what's coming to you" (Revelation 2:20-23, MSG). It is clear from scripture that mean girls, like every other bully will not stop their agenda of harming and eviscerating anyone in their way. But fear not, God, will wipe them from the face of the earth with His divine retribution.

ATHALIAH: Grandmother Shrew Mean Girl

Jezebel and Ahab had children who naturally followed their parent's evil Baal worshiping practices. God's promise through His prophets was exacted just as He said, and Ahab's entire family and Jezebel were blotted out. The dramatic irony of how God's avenging justice against this wicked family unfolded was pure brilliance. God is omnipotent and omniscient which means He is all powerful and all knowing. He knows the end before something has even begun. Human beings, regardless of how crafty or witty they think they are, will never measure up to God. Human brains are infinitely inferior and ridiculously inane compared to God. The smartest thing we as humans can do is accept this fact and to trust, rely and lean on God for everything. He will protect you from all things, known and unknown to you, because He knows everything.

With this in mind, our final mean girl was Athaliah,

daughter of Ahab, king of Israel, and mean girl Jezebel, daughter of Ethbaal, king of Sidonia. Athaliah preserved her mother's evil ways to the letter. She was also as murderous, ambitious, brazen, cruel, scheming, power-hungry, and diabolical as her mother Jezebel. Staying true to Ahab and Jezebel's treacherous repute, Athaliah created royal alliances with the House of Judah, to secure and advance her personal agendas. She married Jehoram, king of Judah, at the same time Athaliah's brother Joram was now king of Israel. This double family alliance in both dynasties; Israel and Judah, ensured that Athaliah would always have unchecked power, wealth, and influence allowing her family to officially enforce Baal worship and conceivably ban the worship of Jehovah God Yahweh in Israel and Judah. The Baal worshipers made it no secret that they intended to corrupt the land and the people and ultimately usurp God from Israel and Judah.

God certainly knew who He was dealing with in this family when He set His face against them, and in the typical fashion of dumb criminals, they dim-wittedly participated in their own demise and were severely and thoroughly vanquished by God almighty. God set in motion His irrevocable plan against Ahab when He spoke these words through His prophet Elijah: "Behold [says the LORD], I am going to bring evil (catastrophe) on you, and will utterly sweep you away, and will cut off from Ahab every male, both bond and free in Israel; and I will make your house (descendants) like that of Jeroboam the son of Nebat, and like the house of Baasha the son of Ahijah, for provoking Me to anger and making Israel sin" (1Kings 21:21-22, AMP).

When Jehoram, son of Jehoshaphat, married Athaliah he created a family relationship with Ahab's unholy family and consequently, his family was brought under the same curse as Ahab. Therefore, when Jehoram succeeded his father Jehoshaphat as king of Judah, and because Jehoram was also wicked, he killed all six of his brothers and some of the leaders of Israel to keep them from trying to take the throne from him, which serendipitously and divinely contributed to the fulfilment of God's sentence to wipe away the house of Ahab. God's divine retribution on Jehoram was very apropos. God sent a letter to Jehoram through the prophet Elijah saying: "Thus says the LORD God of David your father (ancestor): 'Because you have not walked in the ways of your father Jehoshaphat nor in the ways of Asa king of Judah, but have walked in the ways of the kings of Israel, and caused Judah and the inhabitants of Jerusalem to be unfaithful [to God] as the house of Ahab was unfaithful, and you have also murdered your brothers, your father's house (your own family), who were better than you, behold, the LORD is going to strike your people, your sons, your wives, and all your possessions with great disaster; and you will suffer a severe illness, an intestinal disease, until your intestines come out because of sickness, day after day'" (2 Chronicles 21:12-15, AMP). "After about two years he was totally incontinent and died writhing in pain. His people didn't honor him by lighting a great bonfire, as was customary with his ancestors." (2 Chronicles 21:18-19, AMP). Ahaziah (ay-huh-ZYE-uh) became king of Judah when he was 22 years old, after his father Jehoram (jeh-HOR-um) passed away, and only ruled for one year before Jehu struck him down and killed him.

When Athaliah found out Ahaziah had been killed, she murdered all the other royal heirs in a coup d'état, so that she would be the only legitimate successor to Judah's throne. She had no loyalty to the other heirs because Ahaziah was her only son. All the other royal sons were not of her womb so she really didn't care. She was a mean girl, and mean girls will let nothing get in their way of power, dominance and complete control, not even their own blood grandchildren: "When Athaliah the mother of Ahaziah saw that her son was dead, she proceeded to destroy the whole royal family of the house of Judah. But Jehosheba (jeh-HOSH-eh-buh), the daughter of king Jehoram, took Joash (JO-ash) son of Ahaziah and stole him away from among the royal princes who were about to be murdered and put him and his nurse in a bedroom. Because Jehosheba, the daughter of King Jehoram and wife of the priest Jehoida (jeh-HOY-uh-duh), was Ahaziah's sister, she hid the child from Athaliah so she could not kill him. He remained hidden with them at the temple of God for six years while Athaliah ruled the land" (2 Chronicles 22:10-12, NIV).

Eventually this mean girl got exactly what was due to her. After the seventh year of her young grandson Joash's protective custody, Jehoiada the priest, finally got the courage to bring down this bully. He arranged liaisons with the other people of Judah who were on God's side, and swore them to complete loyalty and secrecy. He knew that life and death rested on the shoulders of those in his inner circle and Jehoida probably knew from experience that he could not trust anyone completely. When it comes to evil, power hungry mean girls, they will lie, and distort the truth to ensnare others to loyally follow them. But beware, mean girls are like hungry snakes and will bite you as soon as they have no more use for you. Jehoida and his sons anointed seven-year-old Joash king of Judah. Then the citizens of Judah shouted "Long live the king!" immediately following the coronation. When Athaliah heard all the commotion and saw that Joash was alive and now crowned king, she immediately tried to flex her authority and revoke Joash's ascendancy because she was delusional. She probably thought her loyal henchmen would overthrow the new regime when she loudly cried "Treason!, Treason!" at the young king. Her tactics did not work, and she was quickly seized, taken to the palace's horse stable and killed. After her death, the people of Judah rededicated themselves to God and made a new covenant to be God's special people. They tore down all of the Baal temples and smashed anything associated with Baal. Matta, the detestable priest of Baal was also killed in front of the altar.

In summary, Peninnah, Jezebel and Athaliah were ultimate mean girls who closely and predictably followed a pattern of behavior. By forming 'axes of evil' through repugnant feminine wiles and seduction, they demeaned, harassed, and systematically abolished their competition/targets/victims. Understanding the mean girls twisted mentality assists with taking the most effective actions sooner. If you are the target/victim of a mean girl bully, don't take anything that she does personally. Not to dismiss her ugly behavior in anyway, however, don't credit her actions to something you did or because you lack something. As with most bullies, she is reacting out of her own fears and insecurities. Also, do not believe false reassurances by her or anyone else that "she is not trying to harm you" or that "it is all in your head." If you have already witnessed this monster in action, you are already on notice of what she is capable of doing. If you fall for any of her lies or a persuasive public relations campaign by her followers, you will inevitably be on the losing end of her cutthroat actions. She has no loyalties to anyone. Take the following actions immediately: First, pray and cry out to God for His help in getting rid of her and continue to involve God with every grievance you have. Secondly, remove yourself from her realm or eject her from your realm. If you are unable to extricate yourself from her purview and you know the bullying will continue until you are either completely bashed and thrashed by this person, for step number three, begin a campaign to request assistance. Write letters to people in charge, and carbon copy (cc) the folks in charge of the people in charge. The goal is not to stop at the first tier. Make yourself and this situation known at all levels to keep people accountable. It is unfortunate and disheartening that some people continue to take bullying as, 'not that big a deal', even in the face of studies showing the adverse psychological and physical effects that victims suffer well after the bullying has stopped. So, in order to let those in charge know you mean business and you need relief from this unrelenting mean girl, ensure you create a paper trail starting from the bottom all the way to the top.

TESTIMONY

In 2005/2006 while working for the Administrative Office for the US Courts, I was a government contractor on a team of three when another woman was hired for our team. She was very pretty and very ladylike. She wore the loveliest dresses, and daintiest shoes and her hair was always impeccably coiffed. She wore just the right amount of makeup and always had the sweetest smile on her face. She looked so warm, friendly and inviting I was immediately bedazzled by her. I took her under my wings, trained her, introduced her to everyone and we had lunch together every day. I invited her to my backyard barbeques and she met my husband and daughter, and I even introduced her to my husband's childhood friend. Before I realized what she really was, I was hoodwinked. Not long after, cracks started to form in this syrupy sweet, wouldn't hurt a fly, appearing woman.

For instance, I had a few friends who I would see in passing in the building and I would always make time for a little small talk if I needed to go to their office or if they came to my office. Once, another female coworker stopped by for small talk and a brief "hello, how are you?", and then continued on her way. When the woman left the office, the woman who I thought was so sweet said, "Gosh, she has a big nose!" and frowned her face in disgust. I said, "I never noticed", and also said that she was a nice lady. Nonetheless, I let her comments go unchecked; naïve and unaware that this is how mean girls behave. It wasn't long before this mean girl made me her target. I should have disassociated myself from her when I first saw her ugliness manifest against someone who had never done anything to her. I should have silently told myself that this person was not a nice person and if you know what's good for you, you will extricate yourself as soon as possible. Regrettably, I did not. Not long after, I must have offended the mean girl with one too many of my shielding comments, when she would make harsh comments about others, and I became her target. She made an alliance with a man who we also worked with, as he liked her in a sexual way. It didn't take much for him to be beguiled by her, because he was a horn-dog. Meant to harm me, the mean girl sent our manager an email stating that I was rude and offensive to our customers when they called. She also said that I was rude to her and to others in the office. My manager called me in, and asked me to defend myself against these allegations. The manager would not disclose who said these things. I was completely stumped. In fact, throughout the entire meeting, I referenced the mean girl as a witness and advocate of my innocence. I never thought that she was the person that said these things. My manager was probably thinking I was the biggest idiot on the planet. I was fooled and beguiled by this woman.

My manager told me she would contemplate her decision; however, some kind of reprimand would be forthcoming to me. Later that same day, I was so dejected I just wanted to go home. I prayed and cried out to God in my disgrace and confusion. I could no longer defend myself and I mistakenly thought that one of my male co-workers said those awful things about me. I even confided in the mean girl about the allegations and even told her who I thought it was that said these lies. I was so oblivious and childlike to this type of hate and she acted like she could not believe anything like that was happening to me. She was so evil, she lied with a straight and convincing face.

I ended up staying at work the whole day. I felt like God wanted me to stay and not run away. I had done nothing, so I need not run like a scared animal. Late that evening, one of my other manager's stopped by to say goodnight and pops his head in our office. I was the only one left, since everyone else had gone home. He said to me, "It's such a shame that all of this happened to you, I thought you and 'person's name' were friends." I was completely stunned. This person just revealed that my so-called friend, whom I had really liked as a person because she was pretty, sweet, dainty and feminine, was the one who viciously, cold-heartedly and calculatingly lied on me and put my livelihood and career at risk. I went home and told my family and they consoled me. My fiancé now hubby said it was good that I stayed, because I had done nothing wrong and I had no reason to be going home because of someone's hateful lies.

I don't think I slept that night because of all the turmoil. The next morning, I asked my manager to allow me to speak to her and she agreed. Before I even began to speak, she apologized to me and said, "I didn't sleep well at all last night. Nothing that was said to me about you even made sense. You and 'person's name' were always together, I should have known this was untrue, and I truly apologize about this whole situation." I was so relieved! I thanked God for delivering me and I didn't even have to defend myself. My manager assured me she would deal with the mean girl later that day. However, the mean girl did not even show up to work and didn't call. In fact, she never came back to the office and they ultimately threatened to press charges because she never returned her government issued building access badge. I was totally vindicated! The horn-dog in the office continued to be a snake in the grass, but I now knew who he was. He half-heartedly apologized, but he never had my trust again. I also learned not to overlook ugly behavior by otherwise sweet and feminine women.

"When people show you who they are, believe them the first time."

Maya Angelou

Chapter 4

"For they all wanted to frighten us, thinking, 'They will become discouraged with the work and it will not be done.' But now [O God,] strengthen my hands."

Nehemiah 6:9, AMP

Workplace bullies are maleficent, underhanded co-workers, managers, team leads, supervisors or bosses who go out of their way to make life miserable for another co-worker who they are either in charge of, or is a co-worker who reports to the same boss as they do. The bully perpetuates false propaganda and outright lies for the explicit purpose of undermining and diminishing the target in the eyes of the employer or boss, so that the target looks unqualified, unprepared, under educated, or of dubitable reputation. The bullies select their target based on any false assumption or fear that is within them. The fear could be real or imagined, however the target, in their mind, is perceived as a threat to the bully and he or she wants the boss to feel that the target is not qualified and ultimately keep or place the target in an inferior, submissive or demeaning role under the bully. The target may be fully qualified and also highly competent but the bully will devise many plots and schemes to manipulate a situation to disparage his target. The target must be above reproach and not allow the bully to be proved correct in his smear campaign. The target has to remain vigilant at all times and be careful not to trust the bully in any matter.

Bullies will play on the sensitivities and kindness of their victims, but they really only intend to harm the victim in the end. How does a target deal with this type of workplace predator? By trusting, relying and leaning on God and praying and crying out to Him. God sees this person and He will fight your battles and give you victory.

SANBALLAT & TOBIAH: Sabotaging Workplace Bully Coworkers

Nehemiah (nee-huh-MY-uh), a Jew exiled to Persia, was the victim of some very vicious and unrelenting bullies, who were hell-bent on stopping his endeavors to rebuild Jerusalem's crumbling walls. The walls in Jerusalem were left in ruins as a result of the conquest of the Jews by the Babylonian, King Nebuchadnezzar. Then the Persians defeated the Babylonians. While Nehemiah was serving as the cup-bearer to the Persian king Artaxerxes, he received this word from his family member; "The exile survivors who are left there in the province are in bad shape. Conditions are appalling and the wall of Jerusalem is still in rubble; the city gates are still cinders" (Nehemiah 1:3, MSG). Nehemiah immediately cried out in prayer to God. He asked God for forgiveness for the disobedience of his people, and he asked God for the king's favor so that he would give him permission to go back to Jerusalem to rebuild the wall. When Nehemiah asked the king if he could go back to his homeland and help with the rebuilding efforts, King Artaxerxes agreed to let Nehemiah go, because God was with Nehemiah. God also put it in the king's heart to provide Nehemiah with authorization letters with the king's royal stamp so that Nehemiah would not be stopped or detained at any point on his journey back to Jerusalem. The king also gave Nehemiah a cavalry escort, which is like having the National Guard escort you to your family home in the country. When you include God in your plans prior to making them, He will make your paths straight.

"When Sanballat (san-BAL-at) the Horonite and Tobiah (toh-BYE-uh) the Ammonite official heard about this they were very upset, angry that anyone would come to look after the interest of the People of Israel" (Nehemiah 2:10, MSG). Sanballat and Tobiah were bullies who were also subjects of the Persian king. They were instantly threatened that Nehemiah would gain the king's favor so they began a campaign of devious terror tactics hoping to demoralize Nehemiah and his fellow Jews in their rebuilding efforts. After Nehemiah reached Jerusalem and made the initial inspection of the walls, he motivated his fellow Israelites to begin the work involved. So also began Sanballat and Tobiah's smear campaign of mocking, laughing and jeering at their efforts; "Ha! What do you think you're doing? Do you think you can cross the king?" (Nehemiah 2:19, MSG). Unbeknownst to these two bullies, Nehemiah had already received the king's blessings. This rebuilding effort was not any of their concern, but workplace bullies are always trying to find out what you are working on because they are meddlesome and like to keep strife and rumor stirred up. Nehemiah knew what these bullies were trying to accomplish, and would not let them intimidate him. He replied, "…The God-of-Heaven will make sure we succeed. We're his servants and we're going to work, rebuilding. You can keep your nose out of it. You get no say in this --- Jerusalem's none of your business!" (Nehemiah 2:20, MSG). These workplace bullies like to keep tabs on what you are doing so that they can sabotage with precision. It is difficult to hinder plans that are unknown. Therefore, the sly enemy will come and nose around, inquire of and even follow you, to make sure they know all that you are doing. It's prudent for the victim or target of a workplace bully to understand this and not disclose any non-essential details to this person than what is necessary. To fulfill the mission, oftentimes working closely with a workplace bully is required, but if deceptive practices and sabotage is occurring, it is critically important to immediately remove yourself from their purview and keep a written account of all that is happening. Also, maintain the highest level of excellence, accountability, integrity, and transparency to your superiors so that nothing slanderous said of you will stick. Always be above reproach, and avoid even the appearance of impropriety. "For the eyes of the Lord run to and fro throughout the whole earth to show Himself strong in behalf of those whose hearts are blameless toward Him" (2 Chronicles 16:9, Jub).

Nehemiah adhered to God; therefore, had an excellent character and as such, held the position of cupbearer to the king. The cupbearer is an influential and extremely sensitive position in the king's royal cabinet because he is entrusted with the king's beverages. It was not unheard of for kings to be poisoned, so kings had to have someone extremely trustworthy to serve in this role. The cupbearer also was courageous because he put his life on the line by tasting the king's beverages to make sure it was not poisoned. This said a lot about Nehemiah's character. He lived a courageous, honest, modest, upright, and exemplary life. Irresponsible, ne'er-do-wells have nothing better to do than to start trouble for those that are better than they are. Continue praying out to God, and He will deliver you. Until He fully delivers you, do good and be good.

Nehemiah and his fellow Jews continued working on rebuilding the walls in Jerusalem and they were making outstanding progress. This infuriated their haters all the more: "But when Sanballat heard that we were rebuilding the wall he became furious, completely enraged, and he ridiculed the Jews. He spoke before his brothers and the army of Samaria, 'What are these feeble Jews doing? Can they restore it for themselves? Can they offer sacrifices? Can they finish in a day? Can they revive the stones from the heaps of dust and rubbish, even the ones that have been burned?'" (Nehemiah 4:1-2, AMP). Not only was Sanballat mad and seeing red over something that had absolutely nothing to do with him, now he was vehemently expressing his opinions and venomous comments to a precarious army, the Samarians! This is all indicative of a person who really wants to stop the efforts of another. Why this workplace bully was so enraged is wide-ranging. He could be a lackluster performer and feels that Nehemiah is making him look like the slovenly employee/subject that he really is. Or, perhaps Sanballat has a position of authority, but Nehemiah is on a special project that is unrelated to his realm of authority and does not have to answer to him or provide him with any updates of his progress. Nehemiah reports directly to the king. While Sanballat is raving mad over matters that are not his business, his equally meddlesome sidekick Tobiah chimes in to further harm the Jews by saying, "Even what they are building---if a fox should get up on it, he would break down their stone wall" (Nehemiah 4:3, AMP). His purpose in saying this was to echo the negativity and lend credibility to Sanballat's statements while further destabilizing the Jews efforts at successfully rebuilding the wall. Tobiah's angle was to discredit the value of what the Jews were doing and to gain favor with Sanballat whom he thought would be the victor against the Jews. Being on his side would ensure no repercussions would come his way once Sanballat was in complete authority over the Jews, if that was the expected outcome. But remember, Nehemiah was not even challenging Sanballat. His purpose and mission was only to rebuild those walls; not to fight with a power hungry nobody. The conflict only arose because Sanballat became threatened by activity that had nothing to do with him and would not affect him in any way. Workplace bullies will always use the tactic of discrediting their target with wild, exaggerated or erroneous accusations, and other unsubstantiated deleterious gossip. They want to destabilize their target on multiple fronts; psychologically to get inside the targets mind and poison them from within and on the other front, to plant seeds of doubt in the eyes of those in charge.

Again, to fight against all this opposition, Nehemiah did the only thing that works. He cried out to God in prayer: "Hear us, our God, for we are despised. Turn their insults back on their own heads. Give them over as plunder in a land of captivity. Do not cover up their guilt or blot out their sins from your sight, for they have thrown insults in the face of the builders" (Nehemiah 4:4-5, NIV). Nehemiah doesn't take matters into his own hands and fight the same way these workplace bullies fight. He knows that God will take care of this riffraff and that they will be completely removed from his path. Although Nehemiah was distressed and worried, he knew to give this problem over to God. And he knew that he could keep praying on this same issue, even though he had prayed before. Sometimes it takes repetitive prayer, but that doesn't mean that God did not hear you the first time.

Sometimes evil is so persistent, that you must keep up the fight until it is totally obliterated. A great example of this principle is found in 2 Kings 13:18-19 (NIV), "Then he said, 'Take the arrows,' and the king took them. Elisha told him, 'Strike the ground.' He struck it three times and stopped. The man of God was angry with him and said, 'You should have struck the ground five or six times; then you would have defeated Aram and completely destroyed it. But now you will defeat it only three times.'" This scripture was describing how the prophet

Elisha was prophesying to the king of Israel regarding the outcome of a battle with an attacking army. Elisha told the king to strike the ground, but did not tell him how many times to strike it. The king only struck the ground three times. Elisha becomes upset and said you should have struck the ground five or six times. This tells me that the king was not giving enough effort of what little effort was required of him. All he had to do was hit the ground and that was too much to ask so he gave a piffling "tap, tap, tap." He should have beat that ground over and over till dust clouds formed. If you are truly serious about defeating giants, you need to act like it. Don't be passive and wimpy. Even though God is fighting for you, you have to be a spirited cheerleader with energy and zest. Not deflated, half-hearted or lukewarm or God will spew you out of his mouth; "I know your works, that you are neither cold nor hot: I would you were cold or hot. So then because you are lukewarm, neither cold nor hot, I will spew you out of my mouth" (Revelation 3:15-16, AKJV). Be fired up for God as He fights your battles. We are partners with God, and our human weakness doesn't equate to cowardly. God will do what we can't but your attitude must be in agreement with God who is the Great I AM.

Nehemiah's bully not only tried to intimidate him with words, he also tried to physically harm him so that he could totally stop Nehemiah's efforts. Nehemiah smartly instructed all the workers to post armed guards all along the work site and to be prepared to fight against any person trying to stop them. Since the Jews were now on guard, the workplace bullies resorted to another scheme; to have Nehemiah meet Sanballat and Geshem (GEH-shem), the Arab, in a nearby town. Nehemiah knew it was a trap and didn't take the bait. It's very natural and Christ-like to give people the benefit of the doubt, but unfortunately not everyone deserves such blind trust. Sometimes it is a trap. Unfortunately, in the workplace, you may not have the luxury or authority to opt out of a deceitful meeting. However, you can invite an objective third party to attend with you, so that you don't go headfirst into a sinister trap. Now that Nehemiah outwitted his foes yet again, they did not give up. Sanballat, like Jezebel, composed a letter full of false statements and lies about what Nehemiah was up to, and threatened to send them to the king: "It is reported among the nations and----Geshem says it is true----that you and the

Jews are plotting to revolt, and therefore you are building the wall. Moreover, according to these reports you are about to become their king and have even appointed prophets to make this proclamation about you in Jerusalem: 'There is a king in Judah!' Now this report will get back to the king; so come, let us meet together" (Nehemiah 6:6-7, NIV). Sanballat was so enraged and threatened by Nehemiah, that his twisted mind was determined to stop him at all costs. Geshem was a close chum of Sanballat and his confirmation of what was factual regarding Nehemiah was most unquestionably prejudiced. Again, Nehemiah prayed to God about this latest assault against him, and asked God to give him strength.

When Nehemiah tried to confide in so-called friends, he found out that he could not even trust his friends. They were working with the bully. They even tried to trick Nehemiah into committing a sin that would have jeopardized his reputation. Nehemiah again saw through all of the treachery. He did not fall for any of it. His focus remained on God and finishing the wall. He let God fight his battle while he focused on what he could do which was rebuilding the wall. Nehemiah eventually finished the wall in fifty-two days, despite every plot and every mendacious letter circulated between the nobles and his enemies, meant to spread lies, false propaganda and weaken Nehemiah so that he could not finish the wall. However, the exact opposite happened. Nehemiah was supernaturally strengthened by God, But God, weakened Nehemiah's enemies. They lost their nerve and self-confidence when they realized that the work had been done with the help of God (Nehemiah 6:16, NIV).

HAMAN: Treacherous Workplace Bully

At a time period contemporaneously to our previous giant slayer, Nehemiah, when king Xerxes (ZURK-seez) was ruler over the land, we have the story of Esther and her adoptive father Mordecai (MOR-deh-kye). King "Xerxes ruled over 127 provinces stretching from India to Cush [that is the upper Nile region]: At that time King Xerxes reigned from his royal throne in the citadel of Susa" (Esther 1:1-2). Mordecai was a Jew from the tribe of Benjamin who had been carried into exile from Jerusalem by Nebuchadnezzar (neb-uh-kud-NEZ-er), king of Babylon. "Mordecai had a cousin named Hadassah whom he had brought up because she had neither father nor mother. This young woman, who was also known as Esther, had a lovely figure and was beautiful. Mordecai had taken her as his own daughter when her father and mother died" (Esther 2:7, NIV). The king's wife, Queen Vashti, had become insolent to King Xerxes and publicly embarrassed him. As a result, "The king issued a royal decree that was written in the laws of Persia and Media, which cannot be repealed, that Vashti is never again to enter the presence of King Xerxes. Also let the king give her royal position to someone else who is better than she" (Esther 1:19, NIV). "When the king's order had been publicly posted, many young girls were brought to the palace complex of Susa and given over to Hegai who was overseer of the women. Esther was among them" (Esther 2:8, MSG).

Because Mordecai was older and wiser, he warned Esther to keep her Jewish ethnicity to herself. Esther did as she was told." Esther was gracious and polite and very easy going. Because of her congenial disposition and outward physical beauty, she won the admiration of everyone who saw her. "Hegai liked Esther and took a special interest in her" (Esther 2:9, MSG). "The king fell in love with Esther far more than with any of his other women or any of the other virgins---he was totally smitten by her. He placed a royal crown on her head and made her queen in place of Vashti" (Esther 2:17-18, MSG).

Mordecai usually sat at the King's gate which was a gathering place for men who liked to stay informed of what was going on at the palace. "Esther had not revealed her family or her people [that is, her Jewish background], just as Mordecai had instructed her; for Esther did what Mordecai told her just as when she was under his care" (Esther 2:20, AMP). This secret worked to Mordecai's advantage because while he was sitting at the gate, he overheard a plot to assassinate the king by two of the king's trusted eunuchs, Bigthana and Teresh. "Mordecai told all that he heard to Queen Esther, who then told king Xerxes, giving credit to Mordecai. And when the report was investigated and found to be true, the two officials were impaled on poles. All this was recorded in the book of the annals in the presence of the king" (Esther 2:22-23, MSG, NIV).

After these events, the king promoted Haman to a position of authority in his royal court. Haman was an Agagite, and his people were known to have animosity with the Israelites from ages before when they were called the Amalekites. You read about the "ites" in chapter one *Big Bully Giants*. Haman was now in charge, the "boss man" and he was expecting everyone beneath him to give him his due respect, even those nobles that stood around the King's gate. Mordecai, however, was not going to bow down to anyone who was not the king. He was a Jew, and was only bound to worship God Almighty. He gave the king his respect, however, he was not going to feel compelled to bow down to another man. "All the king's servants who were at the king's gate [in royal service] bowed down and honored and paid homage to Haman; for this is what the king had commanded in regard to him. But Mordecai [a Jew of the tribe of Benjamin] neither bowed down nor paid homage [to him]" (Esther 3:2, AMP). Of course this outraged Haman to no end. And once he found out the reason was because Mordecai was a Jew, he really became indignant. Haman began to scheme to find ways to legally extinguish not just Mordecai, but all Jews throughout the whole kingdom of Xerxes.

Mordecai was wise to tell Esther to keep her ethnicity quiet. Had Haman known what she was, he would have most likely kept his racial prejudices under wraps and worked secretly at trying to harm the Jews and Mordecai. But Haman was a typical bully and probably believed that because he was in charge, he could persuade and or push everyone into going along with the atrocities he had in mind.

So Haman approached the king and spoke falsely about the Jews living in the king's provinces. He told the king that the Jews were odd and they didn't fit in because their ways and customs were different. He lied and said that they disregard the king's laws and told the king that he should not put up with it. Mordecai had disobeyed the king's command by not bowing down to Haman, however the punishment did not fit the crime. Mordecai was not disrespectful to the king nor were the Jews a threat or disrespectful people. Haman lied to advance his objective of eradicating a group of people whom he had a longstanding grudge against. To strengthen his plea to the king, Haman even put 375 tons of silver in the king's bank account to further sway him. The king granted Haman's ruthless request, because on the surface, he only knew what Haman had told him. The king ruled 127 provinces with people from various ethnicities and backgrounds. He had no way of knowing that Haman was planning the demise of a group of people for his own selfish and personal vendetta. Most higher ups, like the king, aren't aware of squabbles that happen beneath them. They are handling high level matters of a global magnitude. When their subordinates come to them regarding the wrangling occurring two levels beneath them, they entrust their direct reports to handle such matters as they see fit. This approach can be most unfortunate when an untrustworthy, power-hungry, workplace bully is supplying their superior with false, deceptive and malicious information meant to undercut and eliminate those who don't have a voice or the boss's ear. But thanks be to God, who knows the end from the beginning. He saw all of this because He is omniscient. He knows all things before they have even manifested. God preordained that Queen Vashti would be banished and divinely made a way for Esther the Jew, to replace her as queen. Even though Queen Esther would risk her life to speak to the king, she was the only hope for God's people to have the ear of the king.

Haman wasted no time in composing and executing his formal death warrants of the Jews in all of the king's provinces. "...The orders were written out word for word as Haman had addressed them to the king's satraps, the governors of every province, and the officials of every people. They were written in the script of each province and the language of each people in the name of King Xerxes and sealed with the royal signet ring. Bulletins were sent out by couriers to all the king's provinces with orders to massacre, kill and eliminate all the Jews---youngsters and old men, women and babies---on a single day, the thirteenth day of the twelfth month, the month Adar, and to plunder their goods" (Esther 3:12-14, NIV). They even publicly posted this edict at the royal palace complex in Susa, which caused a tremendous amount of heartache and overwhelming fear to the Jews living there, and especially to Mordecai.

Mordecai went into a traditional mourning where he tore his clothes and put on sackcloth and ashes and wailed and cried out bitterly. When Queen Esther heard that Mordecai was in distress, she did not know why and summoned her assistant to go to Mordecai to find out what was going on. Mordecai told everything to the assistant and even gave him the words that were written on the posted decree to give to Esther. He told the assistant to ask Esther to go to the king and plead for all of her people's lives. Esther sent a response to Mordecai letting him know that to approach the king without the king granting you admittance with his royal scepter was suicide. Apparently it was a known fact that anyone who approached the king without having this permission granted in advance could be killed for willful disobedience. Mordecai was not trying to hear that. This matter was a life and death situation that needed to be taken care of immediately. Mordecai relayed to Esther, "Do not think that because you are in the king's house you alone of all the Jews will escape. For if you remain silent at this time, relief and deliverance for the Jews will arise from another place, but you and your father's family will perish. And who knows but that you have come to your royal position for such a time as this?" (Esther 4:13-14, NIV).

Esther bravely made the decision to go to the king even in the face of certain death, but she told Mordecai to have all Jews in Susa to fast for her and not eat or drink for three days and nights. She was willing to die doing the right thing for her people. On the third day after the fasting, Esther put on her royal robes and stood in the inner court of the palace, hoping that the king would acknowledge her. He did, and extended his gold scepter that was in his hand. Esther went in and the king asked her what he could do for her. Esther was very careful and chose to finesse her request by inviting the king to a private banquet that she only wanted the king and Haman to attend. This delighted the king because he felt that it was thoughtful and kind of Esther to want to do such a thing. So the king agreed and Esther invited the king and Haman to a second banquet for the next day. In doing it this way, Esther was able to fully prepare for what she wanted to say and say it boldly and without faltering. The king agreed to come to her banquet with Haman the following day.

Haman was over the moon. Being the blowhard that

he was, he thought it was befitting that the queen would want to invite him to any royal shindigs because he was also in charge. In his mind, he was right up there with the king. Later that day, when Haman was still feeling like the king of the world because he was invited to the queens upcoming banquet, he ran into Mordecai at the King's gate. Mordecai still did not bow down to him, and Haman restrained himself but was enraged that Mordecai would not show fear or rise to acknowledge him. When Haman got home, he bragged to his wife and family how the queen invited only him to accompany the king to her banquet. But he said that even this offers him no satisfaction because that Jew Mordecai was still sitting at the King's gate. His brilliant wife and friends told Haman to, "Have a pole set up reaching to the height of fifty cubits, and ask the king in the morning to have Mordecai impaled on it. Then go with the king to the banquet and enjoy yourself. This suggestion delighted Haman, and he had the pole set up" (Esther 5:14, NIV).

God may not be early, but He is always on time. That very night that Haman was plotting to have Mordecai impaled on a pole, the king couldn't sleep. Like most people who have insomnia, they choose a little dry reading to help them fall asleep. The king chose to read the royal log book which had recorded that Mordecai had exposed the assassination conspiracy of Bigthana and Teresh, the two eunuchs who were in close interaction with the king. The king made up his mind that he would honor Mordecai the very next day!

When Haman arrived to the king's court, he was all set to ask the king to impale Mordecai, but before he could even open his mouth to speak, the king presented Haman with a question: "What should be done for the man the king delights to honor? Haman thought to himself, 'He must be talking about honoring me---who else?' So he answered the king, 'For the man the king delights to honor, do this: Bring a royal robe that the king has worn and a horse the king has ridden, one with a royal crown on its head. Then give the robe and the horse to one of the king's most noble princes. Have him robe the man whom the king especially wants to honor; have the prince lead him on horseback through the city square, proclaiming before him, This is what is done for the man whom the king especially wants to honor!'" (Esther 6:6-9, MSG). Boy did Haman royally stick his foot in his mouth or what? He outlined the best tribute ceremony ever, for his arch nemesis

Mordecai. The king loved his idea and told him to go and do all that he said at once for Mordecai the Jew who sits at the King's gate and to not leave out a single detail of your plan. I love God's sense of humor. It is so witty and ingenious and always light years ahead of man's mind.

When Mordecai returned to the king's gate after being publicly honored, Haman ran home in shame and embarrassment. Now Haman's family and friends were singing a new song about how Haman didn't stand a chance if in fact Mordecai was a Jew, since the king was now honoring Mordecai. At that moment, the king's eunuchs arrived to take Haman to Queen Esther's banquet. Haman's day was about to go from bad to really bad.

When Haman arrived, the king asked Esther what was her petition and she boldly asked the king to spare her life and the life of her people. The king was puzzled and a little shocked that she would ask for such a thing. So the queen explained how her people have been scheduled to be destroyed at the end of the year. The king was genuinely not making the connection as to what Esther was talking about. He must have just allowed Haman permission to slaughter a nation without any thought to it whatsoever. The king asked Esther to tell him who it was that was trying to annihilate her people and she said, "An adversary and an enemy is Haman, this evil man. Then Haman became terrified before the king and queen" (Esther 7:16, AMP). The king was furious and left the room to think about what he was going to do. When the king stepped away, Haman tried to grovel to Queen Esther to spare his life, even though he was more than happy to kill her and all the rest of the Jews, without losing an ounce of sleep. When the king returned to the room, he saw that Haman was all over Esther (groveling) while she was on the couch and he became more enraged that Haman would dare to violate his wife when he left the room. The servants immediately placed a hood over Haman's face to prepare him for his execution. One of the eunuchs told the king about the 50-cubit pole that was leaning against Haman's house; the same pole he had set up for Mordecai, who spoke up to help the king. The king ordered them to impale Haman on that very pole.

When the wicked conspire to bring harm and sow evil to those who are weak, God will bring their evil back on their own heads. God is fair and just and He sees how mean and powerful people abuse their authority and He does not like it. Not to be overlooked in this wonderful biblical story in the book of Esther, is the fact that God also delivered His people from a giant bully in the form of an official letter of execution. This type of bully as you may recall from the chapter *Big Bully Giants* typifies a real life and death situation that has the magnitude and destructiveness to decimate your entire life's foundation and bring about ruin. BUT GOD WILL SWEEPINGLY DELIVER THOSE WHO TRUST, RELY, AND LEAN ON HIM FROM ALL DISASTERS!

PHARAOH: Malevolent Bully Boss

"When the wicked are in authority, transgression increases, But the righteous will see the downfall of the wicked" (Proverbs 29:16, AMP). Our next story epitomizes the extreme measures God will take to make a bully leave His people alone. The book of Exodus recounts the story of when the Israelites were great in number and living in Egypt when a new Pharaoh took over after the old one died. The new

Pharaoh did not appreciate the Israelites like his
predecessor had. The Israelites were hardworking,
upstanding, contributing members of their community.
In fact, the Israelites settled in a specific region called
Goshen, where they were shepherds and worked the
land, and enjoyed their quiet pastoral life. They were
fruitful and had many offspring in their families. Their
leader and patriarch Joseph (son of Jacob, son of
Isaac, son Abraham) had recently passed away.
During his life there in Egypt, Joseph was second in
charge to Pharaoh. He was so important in Egypt,
Pharaoh said to Joseph, "I hereby put you in charge of
the whole land of Egypt" (Genesis 41:41, NIV). Joseph
was highly anointed and a gifted prophet of God. God
gave him the ability to interpret dreams. Joseph's rise to
prominence came when he interpreted the dream of
the Pharaoh which ultimately saved the Egyptians from
the widespread famine that ravaged all of the land.
God revealed to Joseph through prophesy that a
famine would come after a time of plenty. God
directed him to stockpile food during the time of plenty
so they would have rations during the famine. Had
Joseph not been there in Egypt, the inhabitants there
and in the surrounding territories would have surely

perished. Egypt had so much food as a result of Joseph's divine wisdom, people from far away would travel to down to Egypt to buy food. And even more incredible is that Egypt had the food to spare. That is quite an accomplishment, however the new Pharaoh either didn't care or didn't know any of this. He was the new man in charge, and he was cleaning house. Unfortunately, many newly appointed managers will come in and make sweeping changes without ever trying to get to know their environment, the way things currently run, who their people are and what motivates them. This is not always a sound approach when acclimating to a new position of authority. Sometimes it helps to sit back and observe and see for yourself how things work. Then make adjustments or overhauls as needed. The excellent workers will appreciate and perhaps buy-in to your recommendations, knowing that you are coming from an informed posture and the subpar employees will get the kick in the pants they've been needing.

The new boss Pharaoh started mistreating and oppressing the Israelites at the onset of his reign. He established overseers and taskmasters over the people to make work arduous, stressful and dangerous. In his backwards thinking, he felt that the Israelites were too numerous and would side with an attacking nation if a war broke out. Typically, when people are happy with their boss, they are very loyal. They don't conspire to overthrow someone who has been kind and generous to them, nor do they take sides with your enemy. This Pharaoh was stupid to say the least. As a result of all his oppression toward the Israelites, not only did it demoralized their esprit de corps, it caused them to reproduce even more. Not sure why that would occur, however this phenomenon caused the Egyptians to dread the Israelites and work them more ruthlessly. This new Pharaoh was also a murderer of innocent babies. He told the midwives, "When you are helping the Hebrew women during childbirth on the delivery stool, if you see that the baby is a boy, kill him; but if it is a girl, let her live" (Exodus 1:16, NIV). When the midwives eluded this unholy request by making up a clever reason why they could not do it, the Pharaoh gave orders to the general public to throw all the boy Hebrew babies in to the Nile, but let every girl live. What a sadistic and evil maniac.

Fortunately, the prophet Moses was born during this turbulent and precarious time and his life was miraculously spared by his quick thinking mother, his precocious older sister and the caring daughter of Pharaoh who happened to be bathing in the Nile when she saw the baby in a basket among the reeds. This king's daughter saved baby Moses and raised him as her own. He was raised and educated in Pharaoh's own palace. He enjoyed everything a young prince was entitled to just as if he was a prince.

When Moses was adult enough to understand all that was occurring with his people being under the despotic thumb of Pharaoh, he did not like what he saw. He tried to take care of things in his own power, however it was not his time to act. Moses was not ready to do all that God had in mind for him to do. However, after a long time away from Egypt in a remote area of the desert, Moses was becoming more mature and humbled so that God could use him to help his people.

God called on Moses and anointed him with the power and authority to take on the ruthless tyrant Pharaoh. Although Moses wasn't confident in himself because of his lack in speaking abilities, he obediently followed

God's call on his life and walked in faith and courage. Moreover, Moses had to convince his own people that it was in their best interest to work with him while he lobbied for their freedom. The Hebrews had become so disheartened by their circumstances under Pharaoh, they were in fear of the unknown to even leave Egypt. This was the only home they had known. And though they were mistreated every day of their lives, they knew no other way. They were institutionalized and had a slave mentality. They were psychologically damaged and didn't know any other way to live. It would be an uphill battle for Moses on every front.

When Moses approached Pharaoh to ask permission for his people to go and worship the God of their ancestors, he was hoping that Pharaoh would be a sensible man and make this process simple and easy. However, Pharaoh scoffed at Moses and questioned his authority. Pharaoh, like many arrogant, overbearing type bosses, did not appreciate anyone he considered inferior to approach him with any bold requests. They prefer someone to approach sheepishly and play the part of a spineless, obsequious, servile employee.

Confidence is regarded as a threat or insult to their authority. Not only did Pharaoh dismiss Moses' authority, he foolishly challenged God's authority; "Who is the LORD, that I should obey him and let Israel go? I do not know the LORD and I will not let Israel go" (Exodus 5:2, NIV). Pharaoh's heart was hardened and God knew Pharaoh would not let His people go without acting like a spoiled tyrant. God wanted to put on a show for His people to build up their confidence since they were so downhearted because of him! God's plan was to demonstrate His supernatural power, wonder and might against the Egyptians, and reveal to His people they could confidently depend on God to fight all of their battles. God was going to beat 'Pharaoh the bully' to a pulp. Pharaoh was such a horrible and repressive boss to the Israelites, he gave orders to the slave drivers and overseers in charge of the people: "You are no longer to supply the people with straw for making bricks; let them go and gather their own straw. But require them to make the same number of bricks as before; don't reduce the quota. They are lazy; that is why they are crying out, 'Let us go and sacrifice to our God.' Make the work harder for the people so that they keep working and pay no attention to lies"

(Exodus 5:6-9, NIV).

Pharaoh would have to learn the hard way just who God is and what God can and will do. Because Pharaoh waffled back and forth and reneged on his word regarding letting the Israelites go on numerous occasions, God ultimately released the following devastating plagues to the Egyptian people:

1. Turned the Nile's water into a putrid, bloody swamp that no one could drink
2. released frogs to overrun the land and dwellings
3. sent swarms of biting gnats (lice) except for land of Goshen
4. sent blood sucking insects to overtake the land and homes except for Goshen
5. caused the Egyptian cattle to die, but not the Israelites
6. caused boils and sores to erupt on man and animals, but not the Israelites
7. caused violent hailstorms that killed man and animals left outdoors except over the land of Goshen
8. sent swarms of migrating locusts to devour all

vegetation

9. covered the land in a blanket of palpable and utter darkness

10. caused death to all first born Egyptian males, man and animal.

"Then the LORD said to Moses, 'Pharaoh will not listen to you, so that My wonders (miracles) may be multiplied in the land of Egypt.' Moses and Aaron did all these wonders (miracles) before Pharaoh; yet the LORD hardened Pharaoh's heart, and he did not let the Israelites go out of his land" (Exodus 11:9-10, AMP). Some of these plagues were a nuisance but some were deadly. All were meant to bring Pharaoh to his senses, but Proverbs 18:6 (AMP) tells us, "A fool's lips bring contention and strife, and his mouth invites a beating." God hardened Pharaoh's heart for the purpose of glorifying God's awesomeness while simultaneously giving the foolish Pharaoh a divine bully beat down!

God is so awesome; not only did He pulverize Pharaoh to surrender, He made the Egyptian people "footstools" to the Israelites as they departed. Psalm 110:1 (AMP) declares: "The LORD (Father) says to my Lord (the Messiah, His Son), Sit at My right hand Until I make Your enemies a footstool for Your feet [subjugating them into complete submission]." The Egyptians were so totally leveled by all the plagues, sickness and death they readily and generously gave the Israelites valuables, money, and clothing just to have the Israelites hastily leave their land. And the Israelites plundered the Egyptians of those things.

Unfortunately, Pharaoh defaulted on his promises yet again, but once more, this was God's divine will to harden Pharaoh's heart, so that God would "be glorified and honored through Pharaoh and all his army...and the Egyptians shall know [without any doubt] and acknowledge that I am the LORD" (Exodus 14:17-18 AMP). Pharaoh had the inhumanity and maliciousness to say "What is this that we have done? We have let Israel go from serving us!" Initially the lying Pharaoh called the Israelites 'lazy and good for nothing', and now he is saying they truly were valuable to him as his servants. Bully bosses are usually evil, exploiting, opportunist and will disparage a good employee and secretly covet them at the same time.

But God faithfully SHOWED up and SHOWED out for His people as He always does. "Then Moses said to the people, 'Do not be afraid! Take your stand [be firm and confident and undismayed] and see the salvation of the LORD which He will accomplish for you today; for those Egyptians whom you have seen today, you will never see again. The Lord will fight for you while you [only need to] keep silent and remain calm'" (Exodus 14:13-14, AMP). So, God separated the Red Sea so that the Israelites could escape, and then He allowed the separated waters to rush upon and drown the Egyptians army who were right behind them in hot pursuit.

Thanks be to God who will beat a bully boss to dust, regardless of your fear, dejection or despair. Sometimes a courageous person like Moses will advocate for you, but more often, you must be your own advocate and go directly to God in prayer and He will hear your cries and rescue you. Also, your enemies will bless you too as you leave that awful situation and embark on a new path leading you to your promised land.

REHOBOAM: Imbecile Bully Boss

Rehoboam (ree-huh-BO-um) was heir and son of King Solomon, and grandson of King David. He ruled over Israel after his father passed away. Because of King Solomon's sins, God had decided to tear the kingdom of Israel in two. Solomon's disobedience to God caused him to forget God's commands not to intermarry with the surrounding nations which would cause Israel to sin.

> King Solomon, however, loved many foreign women besides Pharaoh's daughter---Moabites, Ammonites, Edomites, Sidonians and Hittites. They were from nations about which the LORD had told the Israelites, "You must not intermarry with them, because they will surely turn your hearts after their gods." Nevertheless, Solomon held fast to them in love. He had seven hundred wives of royal birth and three hundred concubines, and his wives led him astray. As Solomon grew old, his wives turned his heart after other gods, and his heart was not fully devoted to the LORD his God, as the heart of David his father had been. He followed

Ashtoreth the goddess of the Sidonians, and
Molek the detestable god of the Ammonites.
Solomon did evil in the eyes of the LORD; he did
not follow the LORD completely, as David his
father had done (1 Kings 11:1-6, NIV).

Solomon was blessed with extreme wealth and wisdom
by God. But like all humans who sin and fall short, he
disobeyed God and consequently forgot God's words
and did all the abominable things that God warned
him not to do. Unlike David his father, Solomon did not
repent and turn away from his sins. He continued on in
his recklessness until it was too late. Once Solomon
died, his doltish son Rehoboam was now in charge.
Rehoboam was asked by his people to consider
reducing their work load because his father had
placed on them an extremely heavy yoke of hard
labor. The people were happy to work for Rehoboam,
just as they had happily served Solomon, but wanted to
have better working conditions. Instead of Rehoboam
carefully considering what they requested, he foolishly
took the advice and counsel of his childhood buddies
over the wiser advice of the elders and respected
leaders as to what he should do. The young men
stupidly advised Rehoboam to crush the people even

more. So he unwisely threatened the workers, saying that since Solomon terrorized them with whips, he would scourge them with scorpions (whips with sharp metal studs). The people threw up their hands, and rejected Rehoboam as their king, having no more to do with him. The kingdom was divided and Rehoboam was left with only one tribe of the twelve original tribes of Israel.

Some bosses are a detriment to themselves as well as those under them because they are megalomaniacs. Instead of cooperating, they feel that they are godlike and see themselves as such. It takes an eye-opening experience such as an insurrection or schism in the workplace before these despots understand and realize that not everybody is going to take being treated unkindly. Foolishly, these type of bully bosses will resort to vindictive hostilities towards subordinates to show them who is in control. So too did Rehoboam. In his inane mind, Rehoboam thought it wise to go to war against his fellow Israelites who decided to withdraw from him. But God told Rehoboam through the prophet Shemaiah (sheh-MY-uh) "Do not go up to fight against your brothers, the Israelites. Go home, every one of you, for this is my doing" (1 Kings 12:24, NIV). Nonconformed, Rehoboam then tried to protect his paltry power by building alliances and strongholds: "Rehoboam continued to live in Jerusalem but built up a defense system for Judah all around..." (2 Chronicles 11:5, MSG). When a bully starts to feel their power slipping, they desperately want to get it back. They will make devious and underhanded deals with others who are corrupt to support and aid their quest for power. BUT GOD, will humble those who try to set aside what is good in favor of embracing evil: "By the time Rehoboam had secured his kingdom and was strong again, he and all Israel with him, had virtually abandoned God and His ways" (2 Chronicles 12:1, MSG) so God sent a mighty army from Egypt as punishment. Rehoboam immediately humbled himself and God magnanimously and quickly forgave Rehoboam and did not allow the Egyptians to utterly abolish them, but he did put them under the Egyptians rule for a time. Isn't it delightful to know that our GOD will not allow a haughty, self-righteous, self-serving bully to remain in a position of authority very long? They may serve for a time, BUT GOD will eventually remove them.

"For yet a little while and the wicked one will be gone [forever]; Though you look carefully where he used to be, he will not be [found]" (Psalm 37:10, AMP).

TESTIMONY

I've experienced plenty of bully bosses in the work place as well as a few coworker bullies. I'm very pleased to share a story of someone who I was able to help who was the victim of a coworker bullying situation. The young lady victim was new to our company and was receiving on the job training (OJT) from a long time employee who was very knowledgeable of our analytical processes. The manager preferred to have other coworkers gain valuable supervisory experience by letting them be in charge of bringing a new employee up to speed. This is a great opportunity for those who know a lot to also gain leadership skills and help a fellow coworker learn critical aspects of the job. However, it was not a good pairing of these two people. Not so much the new employee, but the seasoned employee was not very patient or kind to the new employee. She would actually taunt the new employee when she felt the new employee wasn't quite learning up to her expectations. She would "pop-quiz" her with questions and if the new employee would get it wrong or hesitate too long, the seasoned employee would say things like, "If this is too hard for you, let me know and I'll see if we can place you in another department" or "You're not smart enough to do this type of work." She was so hurtful to the new employee but the new employee never told the manager. The experienced employee was highly skilled and had a longstanding personal friendship with the manager. In fact, they belonged to the same sorority and would often speak of this in the workplace, and of how long they'd known each other. Because of these things, the new employee felt that the manager would most likely believe anything negative the veteran employee said about her as the gospel truth. I had no idea anything like this was going on and I would occasionally see or talk to the new employee over the phone or have lunch with her at our office and assist her in any way I could. I was also a veteran employee, and for a long time performed the same type of work that she was now learning. I was not in her group, so I could not train her. One day while on a phone call with her, I asked her how she was progressing in her OJT and she despondently confided in me how badly things were going between her and the other employee. She was overcome with anguish and sadness and she said she wanted to leave her job. She was not sleeping at night and she was always crying and afraid of any interaction she had to have with the other lady. I couldn't believe what I was hearing. I was so sad for her, and I asked if she had told the manager these things. She said that the manager seemed to be aware of how the other employee was treating her. She also felt that the manager was already on the side of the other employee because of their personal friendship. I told her none of that matters and it was unacceptable that she was being tormented and had not said anything. I told her I could not stand by, knowing what I know and not do anything about it. I also warned her that if we don't make the manager aware and put her on notice of what is going on, we can't expect a change. But If we tell the manager, and she permits this tormenting situation to continue, that it would be negligent on her part and the manager would be held administratively and legally accountable if she then escalated her grievance and put in a formal grievance. She was afraid and really downhearted over her situation. I was resolved to say something, so I brought the matter up to the manager in confidence and consideration of the new employee's fear regarding the manager's potential partiality. The manager at first tried to brush it off as not being that bad. But I persisted and told her that training should not humiliate, taunt, terrorize or victimize anyone. Nor should it stress someone to the point where they are not sleeping and feeling frightened at every interaction. This is grounds for immediate intervention. I also warned her, that as a manager she would have culpability if this workplace bully situation (that she was aware of, and did nothing to intervene) caused adverse ramifications, whether at work or off work. The manager finally agreed and said she would remove the new employee from under the veteran employee and work with the new employee exclusively. The new employee was elated and relieved that she was out from under that bully. She was now happy and was able to learn her job better than ever. Within two months the new employee had analyzed a case so successfully that she uncovered a significant, "smoking-gun" finding that proved crucial to a very high profile case. Within a month of all that happened, the new employee was put in for an award as a result of her outstanding work. The manager called me to tell me about the award for the new employee and she thanked me for speaking up for the employee. She said had it not been for me speaking up for her, she would have most likely stayed under that bully and continued to be tormented without a voice. I'm very happy that I spoke up for my friend. I would want someone to do the same for me. No one should be tormented by anyone. We are all God's children and He doesn't like us to be hurt by others and He will help you. My friend cried out to me, and God operated through me to help her. God will help you no matter where you are, so just reach out in any way you can and He will hear you. Don't suffer in silence.

Chapter 5

When the righteous cry for help, the Lord hears and delivers them out of all their troubles. The Lord is near to the brokenhearted and saves the crushed in spirit. Many are the afflictions of the righteous, but the Lord delivers him out of them all. He keeps all his bones; not one of them is broken.

Psalm 34:17-20, ESV

Schoolyard bullies can best be described as individuals that have a habit of attacking individuals who are already in the midst of a crisis or under attack and can't (or are powerless to) stand up for, defend or protect themselves or their belongings. Schoolyard bullies can be children, young adults, or fully grown adults but are labeled as such due to their immature and unkind cruelty. These bullies, like other types of bullies already discussed, do not know how to behave in a civilized society.

Schoolyard bullies will attack as a group to inflict their acts of cruelty similarly to a mob mentality or a "Lord of the Flies" mentality. As they are committing these shocking and heartless acts they rabble-rouse others like them to carry on the brutality until the defenseless prey has been completely battered and abused or left for dead. Because everyone participated, they somehow justify their behavior and never feel the slightest disgrace or contrition. But our Father in Heaven sees this as an abomination and will not allow this atrocity to go unpunished.

The CHALDEANS; Babylonian Astrologers and KING NEBUCHADNEZZAR

The Israelites had since been displaced from their homeland of Israel because of continual unrepentant disobedience which included worshiping other gods, idolatry, practicing divination, astrology, bowing down to celestial objects and doing what the surrounding nations did. During the reign of King Josiah, when the Israelites were still in their own land, the Book of the Law of Moses was found in the temple of God that was built by Solomon. King Josiah had his secretary read to him what was in the book and learned that Israel had been on a reckless path of destruction for a long time. Josiah said, "Great is the LORD's anger that burns against us because those who have gone before us have not obeyed the words of this book; they have not acted in accordance with all that is written there concerning us" (2 Kings 22:13, NIV). As a result, God predetermined their exile from Israel and banished them to Babylon to live among those people who regularly and customarily worshiped many other gods, celestial objects, practiced sorcery, fortunetelling, and all types of divination. All the things the Israelites would not stop doing.

At this time, The Babylonian King Nebuchadnezzar, was the mightiest king in the land. He had ruthlessly conquered countless other nations who could not withstand his powerful army. King Nebuchadnezzar was a narcissistic despot filled with pride and self-righteousness. He felt that everything and everyone should worship him or his likeness above anything, including God, Creator of the Universe. He was so full of himself, he didn't even know there was only one true God. He actually thought it was by his might and power that the world existed and that he was the absolute ruler over all creation. Nebuchadnezzar's egomania was beyond redemption. Just before God humbled and completely laid Nebuchadnezzar low, this is what Nebuchadnezzar arrogantly said: "Is not this the great Babylon I have built as the royal residence, by my mighty power and for the glory of my majesty" (Daniel 4:30, NIV).

Prior to this aforementioned event whereby God humiliated and downgraded Nebuchadnezzar, the foolish king made a gold-plated image of himself for the purpose of having all his captives and subjects bow down and worship it. Then he made it an official ordinance throughout the land that was strictly enforced by all his officials and henchman. A town crier went about declaring this message to all the people: "Attention, everyone! Every race, color, and creed, listen! When you hear the band strike up---all the trumpets and trombones, the tubas and baritones, the drums and cymbals---fall to your knees and worship the gold statue that King Nebuchadnezzar has set up. Anyone who does not kneel and worship shall be thrown immediately into a roaring furnace" (Daniel 3:4-6, MSG).

A group of Chaldeans (kal-DEE-unz) also known as Babylonian astrologers wanted to make trouble for three God-fearing Israelites; Shadrach, Meshach, and Abednego who would not bow down to this image because it was against their faith in God Jehovah YAWEH to do such a thing. The Israelites had already blasphemed God and were unfaithful and that was why they were in their current situation in Babylon. God was so displeased with their wanton disregard for Him, even after He tried many times to get them to turn away from their disgusting sins of idolatry, worshiping other gods, practicing pagan religion and all sorts of abominable things. But these three men were not going to do anything to upset God Almighty. They were doing everything they could to show reverence and repentance, to quickly gain God's forgiveness and return to their homeland of Israel. It was clear that King Nebuchadnezzar thought highly of them because the astrologers made it a point to say that they were in high positions: "They said to King Nebuchadnezzar, 'Long live the king! You gave strict orders, O king, that when the big band started playing, everyone had to fall to their knees and worship the gold statue, and whoever did not go to their knees and worship it had to be pitched into a roaring furnace. Well, there are some Jews here---Shadrach, Meshach, and Abednego--- whom you have placed in high positions in the province of Babylon. These men are ignoring you, O king. They don't respect your gods and they won't worship the gold statue you set up'" (Daniel 3:8-12, MSG). Why would these astrologers feel so personally concerned with what three Israelites captive were doing? It was because they were green with envy and jockeying for a higher position than what they had. These Israelites were a threat to them so the astrologers put targets on their backs so that they could eliminate them and move up higher to their soon to be vacant positions. Their wicked plan was working as planned because King Nebuchadnezzar immediately and furiously interrogated them. "Is it true, Shadrach, Meshach, and Abednego, that you don't respect my gods and refuse to worship the gold statue that I have set up? I'm giving you a second chance---but from now on, when the big band strikes up you must go to your knees and worship the statue I have made. If you don't worship it, you will be pitched into a roaring furnace, no questions asked. Who is the god who can rescue you from my power?" (Daniel 3:13-15, MSG). Nebuchadnezzar actually thought that he was greater than anything on heaven or earth.

Shadrach, Meshach and Abednego were very bold and brave and did not flinch. They told King Nebuchadnezzar that they would not be forced to worship any images. Furthermore, they said, "Your threat means nothing to us. If you throw us in the fire, the God we serve can rescue us from the roaring furnace and anything else you might cook up, O king.

But even if he doesn't, it wouldn't make a bit of difference, O king. We still wouldn't serve your gods or worship the gold statue you set up" (Daniel 3:16-18, MSG). Trusting in God will require courage. Please understand that even when you are trembling and fearful, while you are trusting in God you can do all things. He will supernaturally empower you to do all things.

Remember when the Israelites were about to cross into the promised land of Canaan and had to fight all those nations and the Nephilim giants? Right before they crossed into the land, God gave Joshua a very stern pep talk and repeated THREE times for Joshua to be bold and very courageous: Joshua 1:6, AMP: "Be strong and confident and courageous, for you will give this people as an inheritance the land which I swore to their fathers (ancestors) to give them", Joshua 1:7, AMP: "Only be strong and very courageous…" and again in Joshua 1:18, AMP: "Any man who rebels against your command and does not obey everything that you command him, shall be put to death; only be strong and courageous." God will fight our battle with **HIS** mighty power and strength, but He requires our faith and our faith requires our action of doing things in the face of our fear. That is what courage is: doing what is frightening, while disregarding your fear. Don't let fear stop you because God is going to give you the victory. God has a long history of telling His people to be of good courage: In 2 Chronicles 32:7 (NIV) God tells the Israelites, "Be strong and courageous. Do not be afraid or discouraged because of the king of Assyria and the vast army with him, for there is a greater power with us than with him." Again God tells His people in 2 Chronicles 20:15 (NIV) why they should be courageous: "He said: 'Listen, King Jehoshaphat and all who live in Judah and Jerusalem!' This is what the Lord says to you: 'Do not be afraid or discouraged because of this vast army. **For the battle is not yours, but God's. You will not have to fight this battle**. Take up your positions; stand firm and see the deliverance the LORD will give you, Judah and Jerusalem. Do not be afraid; do not be discouraged. Go out to face them tomorrow and the LORD will be with you.'" What a mighty God we serve. He will do all the hard stuff, all we have to do is show up and be in a state of readiness; showing courage and strength. Even though you may be afraid, DO NOT have a deportment of self-doubt and defeat.

Shadrach, Meshach and Abednego did exactly what

God wanted them to do; they showed courage in the face of fear. They stood bravely, having no idea if God would give them victory or not, but showing no fear. King Nebuchadnezzar and his sycophant astrologers tried to intimidate them, but they did not cringe or tremble. They stood firm with an intrepid posture and told the bully king "We do not need to defend ourselves before you in this matter. If we are thrown into the blazing furnace, the God we serve is able to deliver us from it, and He will deliver us from Your Majesty's hand. But even if He does not, we want you to know, Your Majesty, that we will not serve your gods or worship the image of gold you have set up" (Daniel 3:16-18, NIV). God loves when we boldly declare His goodness and His might. He relishes it so much because it works with God's omnipotence and galvanizes all of

His awesome power, compounded with our faith, to exact perfect defeat against the enemy of those who trust, rely, and lean on Him.

True to the bully code of conduct, Nebuchadnezzar became infuriated and outraged because the men boldly spoke the truth to him. Who did they think they were anyway? He was the king of the world, so he thought. Like many bullies, Nebuchadnezzar also exhibited emotional instability evinced by his mercurial mood swings; "His attitude toward them changed. He ordered the furnace heated seven times hotter than usual and commanded some of the strongest soldiers in his army to tie up Shadrach, Meshach and Abednego and throw them into the blazing furnace. So these men, wearing their robes, trousers, turbans and other clothes, were bound and thrown into the blazing furnace" (Daniel 3:19-22, NIV). Because Nebuchadnezzar was a typical hot-headed tyrant, he didn't quite think things through. In his haste to punish these innocent men, he caused harm to his own men who were acting on his knee-jerk orders; "Because the king's command was urgent and the furnace was extremely hot, the flames of the fire killed the men who carried up Shadrach, Meshach, and Abednego" (Daniel 3:23, AMP). BUT GOD, delivered the three men in SHOCK and AWE. To the amazement and astonishment of all who witnessed, "Suddenly King Nebuchadnezzar jumped up in alarm and said, 'Didn't we throw three men, bound hand and foot, into the fire?...But look!', he said. 'I see four men, walking around freely in the fire, completely unharmed! And the fourth man looks like a son of the gods!'" (Daniel 3:24-25, MSG). This is a very valuable message for all who have been the target of bullies of any type. God allows us to go through some measure of torment, not to punish us, though we momentarily suffer the tormenting effects of the bully. God uses these situations to SHOW UP and SHOW OUT; magnifying His GLORY and GREATNESS through our circumstances. Just like when God showed His greatness to the Egyptians through His magnificent signs, majestic miracles and awesome wonders to show **unbelievers** HIS GREATNESS. "He struck down the firstborn of Egypt, the firstborn of people and animals. He sent his signs and wonders into your midst, Egypt, against Pharaoh and all his servants" (Psalm 135:8-9, NIV). And our Lord and Savior Jesus Christ said, "Unless you people see signs and wonders," Jesus told him, "you will never believe" (John 4:48, NIV).

Trusting in God has transcending rewards: in addition to magnifying God's goodness and glorifying His name, He will not only remove you from that dire situation because of your faithfulness, He will as an extra bonus, frustrate and stupefy your enemies by ridding you of any deleterious or residual effects of their abuse. "Nebuchadnezzar went to the door of the roaring furnace and called in, 'Shadrach, Meshach, and Abednego, servants of the High God, come out here!' Shadrach, Meshach, and Abednego walked out of the fire. All the important people, the government leaders and king's counselors, gathered around to examine them and discovered that the fire hadn't so much as touched the three men---not a hair singed, not a scorch mark on their clothes, not even the smell of fire on them!" (Daniel 3:26-27, MSG). HALLELEUJAH! GLORY BE TO GOD ALMIGHTY! THEY DID NOT EVEN SMELL LIKE SMOKE! WHAT A GOOD GOD WE SERVE! Last but not least, God will promote you too; another blessing for your faithfulness: "Nebuchadnezzar responded and said, 'Blessed be the God of Shadrach, Meshach, and Abednego, who has sent His angel and rescued His servants who believed in, trusted in, and relied on Him! They violated the king's command and surrendered their bodies rather than serve or worship any god except their own God. Therefore I make a decree that any people, nation, or language that speaks anything offensive against the God of Shadrach, Meshach, and

Abednego shall be cut into pieces and their houses be made a heap of rubbish, for there is no other god who is able to save in this way!'" (Daniel 3:28-29, AMP). "Then the king promoted Shadrach, Meshach and Abednego in the province of Babylon" (Daniel 3:30, NIV). The Chaldeans astrologers worst fear was realized when they foolishly decided to pick on people who trusted, relied and leaned on God. Anyone who foolishly chooses to victimize God's faithful children, will assuredly suffer God's divine retribution in a sudden and devastating spectacle.

In a grand gesture that only our wonderful and magnificent God could perform, the arrogant, evil King Nebuchadnezzar was finally and forever broken down and laid low. After seeing how God defended three of His servants, Shadrach, Meshach and Abednego, Nebuchadnezzar continued to behave like a conceited blowhard. One day while he was walking on the terrace of his royal palace, Nebuchadnezzar started to speak arrogantly; "Look at this, Babylon the great! And I built it all by myself, a royal palace adequate to display my honor and glory!" No sooner had the words left his mouth, God spoke to him from heaven and said "This is the verdict on you, King

Nebuchadnezzar: Your kingdom is taken from you. You will be driven out of human company and live with the wild animals. You will eat grass like an ox. The sentence is for seven seasons, enough time to learn that the High God rules human kingdoms and puts whomever he wishes in charge" (Daniel 4:30-32, MSG). At once, Nebuchadnezzar was driven mad, and lived in the wild among animals. His hair grew like feathers of an eagle and his nails grew like talons of a hawk.

Nebuchadnezzar was now like the wild beasts who walked on all fours. At the end of the seven years, he came back to his right and stable mind, and was given back the majesty and splendor he once had. But now he was giving all honor, glory and praise to God Almighty. No longer was Nebuchadnezzar a pompous, arrogant king who thought so highly of himself. He now acknowledged the one true God of heaven and earth by saying "Now I, Nebuchadnezzar, praise and exalt and glorify the King of heaven, because everything He does is right, and all His ways are just. And those who walk in pride He is able to humble" (Daniel 4:37, NIV).

BULLIES Who Conspired Against Daniel

Continuing where we left off with Shadrach, Meshach and Abednego, we have the story of Daniel. Like his Jewish relatives already mentioned, Daniel was an upstanding, God-fearing man who was diligent in all his duties. He reverently served God without wavering or doubt above anyone or anything. Because the Jewish people had already sinned against God so severely when they were still in Israel, God punished His people by allowing them to become captives of the Babylonians. King Nebuchadnezzar was now dead and his descendant Belshazzar took over. Belshazzar did what King Nebuchadnezzar did and was arrogant and foolish. As a result, he was slain by King Darius the Mede

who took down the Babylonian empire and brought their Persian empire to rule over Babylon.

Darius established and appointed 120 governors over the citizens in all of his provinces. And he placed three vice-regents over all the governors, and Daniel was one of them. Although Daniel was an exiled Jew from Israel, he was highly regarded as one of king Darius's trusted official. This was because Daniel was faithful and trustworthy in all that he did. He was obedient to God, and God blessed him with wisdom and discernment to know things that not even the Babylonian astrologers or magicians or fortunetellers could ever know. The Babylonian astrologers, magicians and fortunetellers received recognition and prominent standing because they spoke false predictions and pretended to interpret signs and dreams of the leaders and the kings. But they were all fake. They knew much of nothing and it became evident in every situation that they were called upon to interpret. But Daniel proved himself to be truly gifted by God to understand and know very difficult things. He was called upon by King Nebuchadnezzar one year before he was driven into

the wilderness to understand what his dream meant. Daniel was also called upon by Belshazzar to interpret signs that were written on the kings wall. With each of Daniel's interpretation, Daniel told his superiors that God is the only one that can reveal and give understanding to what their dreams or what the signs meant. Daniel never let anyone think that he was doing this of his own power. He gave all honor and glory to God Almighty. Those phony astrologers, magicians and fortunetellers never did that. They did not know God and became very jealous of Daniel and his divine abilities. And now his fellow vice-regents were jealous of Daniel too; "But Daniel, brimming with spirit and intelligence so completely outclassed the other vice-regents and governors that the king decided to put him in charge of the whole kingdom" (Daniel 6:3, MSG). Then the other vice-regents began to try and find a reason to bring charges against Daniel in his conduct of government affairs, but they could not find any corruption in him. So they wickedly conspired to use Daniel's obedience to God against him.

Daniel's wicked coworkers surreptitiously went to the king behind Daniel's back and talked him into creating a new law that said that the people could pray only to the king for the next thirty days and not to anything or anyone else, not even God. "The royal administrators, prefects, satraps, advisers and governors have all agreed that the king should issue an edict and enforce the decree that anyone who prays to any god or human being during the next thirty days, except to you, Your Majesty, shall be thrown into the lions' den. Now, Your Majesty, issue the decree and put it in writing so that it cannot be altered---in accordance with the law of the Medes and Persians which cannot be repealed. So King Darius put the decree in writing" (Daniel 6:7-9, NIV).

When Daniel learned of this new decree, he continued to pray to God three times a day as he always did. Daniel knew this was an evil and unlawful decree, even though he was obedient to the king, he could not be obedient to the king and disobey God if he followed this order. Daniel rightly chose to obey God. Those wicked coworkers followed Daniel home in order to catch him praying. When they did find him praying as

he normally did, not hiding it at all, they immediately reported back to King Darius what Daniel had been found doing. "So they went to the king and spoke to him about his royal decree: "Did you not publish a decree that during the next thirty days anyone who prays to any god or human being except to you, Your Majesty, would be thrown into the lions' den? The king answered, 'The decree stands---in accordance with the law of the Medes and Persians, which cannot be repealed" (Daniel 6:12, NIV).

Like all jealous bullies, the coworkers now tried to use something negative against him: "Daniel, who is one of the exiles from Judah, pays no attention to you, Your Majesty, or to the decree you put in writing. He still prays three times a day" (Daniel 6:13, NIV). Reminding the king that Daniel was an exile was just another jab to undermine Daniel. They could have easily said that "He is your trusted servant" or "Daniel, the one who has been honorable, and trustworthy in all his duties." But no; they chose to try and use something that would make him seem unworthy, or deserving of being mistreated. However, King Darius felt just the opposite;

he was greatly distressed that he had enacted that decree. He honestly had no idea that those wicked coworkers were manipulating him. "When the king heard this, he was greatly distressed; he was determined to rescue Daniel and made every effort until sundown to save him" (Daniel 6:14, NIV). So the coward bullies went to King Darius as a group to remind him that Daniel had to be put in the lions' den. So Darius reluctantly allowed his officials to carry out this wicked decree, even though it hurt him to bring harm to Daniel. Darius even gave Daniel his most sincere blessings; "May your God, whom you serve continually, rescue you!" (Daniel 6:16, NIV).

Daniel was locked in with those lions right away and the king finalized the sentence by sealing the order with his signet ring. Daniel's fate was now immutable by anyone. BUT GOD, supernaturally shut the mouths of the lions in the den and they did not raise a paw to hurt Daniel, Hallelujah!

King Darius was so distraught when he left Daniel in the lions' den, he went to bed without food or drink and did not allow himself any form of entertainment. He was

in anguish at all that was transpiring with Daniel. He knew his officials had concocted this wicked scheme just to get rid of Daniel and he allowed it because he was not paying attention to what was happening right under his nose. At the crack of dawn, the next morning, King Darius immediately went to Daniel and called for him in the lions' den. "Daniel, servant of the living God, has your God, whom you serve continually, been able to rescue you from the lions? Daniel answered, 'May the king live forever! My God sent His angel, and he shut the mouths of the lions. They have not hurt me, because I was found innocent in His sight. Nor have I ever done any wrong before you, Your Majesty'" (Daniel 6:20-23, NIV). Darius was so elated that Daniel was unharmed that he ordered him to be let out of the den. Just like Shadrach, Meshach and Abednego did not smell like smoke, Daniel had not a scratch on him when he emerged from the lions' den! God will make the wicked look like idiots when He rescues His people from their wicked conspiracies. What they planned for harm, will not only not harm you, but set you up for victory.

The king ordered those who falsely accused Daniel to be thrown into the lions' den along with their wives and children. Before they could make it all the way in, the lions attacked and devoured them. Then King Darius canceled his previous decree and replaced it with a new decree stating, "I issue a decree that in every part of my kingdom people must fear and reverence the God of Daniel. For he is the living God and He endures forever; His kingdom will not be destroyed, His dominion will never end. He rescues and He saves; He performs signs and wonders in the heavens and on the earth. He has rescued Daniel from the power of the lions" (Daniel 6:26-27). And Daniel continued to prosper under the reign of Darius and the reign of his successor Cyrus.

Daniel, Shadrach, Meshach and Abednego were all careful and obedient to God's word. They valued God's laws and decrees above man's. Their obedience gave them a supernatural anointing and protection from God. They were insulated from the fowler's snare and a trap that the wicked set for their victims. Obedience to God will keep you from being a victim to these evildoers. The wicked schemes of these bullies came down on their own heads because they were evil and God will snuff out the wicked in due time.

TESTIMONY

I had just started a new job and thought I hit the jackpot. It was a great job, with more opportunity to learn and grow within the always expanding Information Technology and Cyber Security realm. There is always a need for those who know and understand this industry. When I arrived for my first day, I was instantly met with a cold wall of hostility. The atmosphere, the employees, all seemed mad or depressed. Looking back, I was probably a little too bubbly for these angry people.

At that time, I was a babe in Christ and didn't quite know or understand much of God's word and how His word has power. But going through the hard times I'm about to tell you, really pushed me closer to God. What I didn't know was that my co-workers had recently undergone a change in management. The previous manager, who was much beloved, retired. The new manager was the typical 'new sheriff in town', and was shaking things up and they did not like it. So, looking back, it wasn't that they didn't like me, but I didn't really help. In fact, they wrongly thought that I was brought in to replace another of their beloved co-workers who left on pretty bad terms when the new manager took over. So they believed that the new manager was systematically replacing the old, stale regime with 'fresh' new employees.

I was completely cold-shouldered by my co-workers. Whenever we had offsite functions to celebrate retirements, or holidays, no one talked to me. I tried to break the ice, I smiled, I chimed into the conversations and they would completely talk past me and would not even make eye contact. It was as if I was invisible to them. I didn't understand what was happening so I would try again, thinking it wasn't what it seemed. But even in the office, I would notice that I would not be greeted in return when I spoke in the mornings. Things got so bad that my co-worker who I was directly tasked to shadow would deliberately not give me information or would provide me with inaccurate or false information.

It finally came to a head when he said to me, "At your level, you should already know how to do such and such. If you don't, I'm not gonna help you." That was it! I finally told him, "We don't have to like each other, but you will respect me." I also said I would be willing to start over from scratch if he was willing. He did not relent in his nastiness, so I finally got it through my head that he and everyone else just didn't like me, and I would no longer try to befriend them. I would do my work with assistance from others who were not immature and mean. That worked out just fine. I found out much later down the line why they behaved so terribly to me and learned that those bullies were a part of a clique of embittered, near-retirement employees who believed the company no longer valued them, so they despised new employees, especially those who appeared young, spritely and happy about life. I fit that description.

I am very happy to say that I did not let them affect me with their meanness. I took all my woes to God and He protected me and got me through this hard time. Five years later, the co-worker who said, "At your level…", was the one who called and told me about the new job opportunity that was announced and I ultimately got that job. He was my footstool. Won't God make your enemies your footstool? Yes, He will.

<u>TESTIMONY</u>

During the same time as the previously mentioned testimony, the new manager was an equal opportunity tormentor. He seemed to take pleasure in baiting all of his employees into arguments so that he could amuse himself with what he thought was his logic and wit which I found to be completely incomprehensible. He sadistically spoke entirely in riddles for his own twisted amusement and to confound his subordinates. But in actuality he was a blowhard and the best thing to do was to say as little as possible and to avoid any kind of debate. Even if he invited your feedback, it was learned by plenty of prior setups, not to take his bait. This manager was the one I will credit with drawing me ever closer to God.

Every day on my way to work, I would pray to God and ask for His protection and mercy before going into the office and loudly rebuke the devil. This manager seemed to go out of his way to try and stomp on my self-esteem, my work product, my skills and my abilities. He even downgraded my performance report when he went above and beyond to find fault with me regarding a missed deadline. I had been in an intense technical training for two weeks, and during the time I was away, a directive from our administrative department came down, that required everyone to take a specific action by a specific date. Because I was in training, I didn't complete the action until my first day back to work. Well this manager had been eagerly watching and waiting to see if I had made the deadline. I missed it. No big deal, I did it very soon afterwards. That was not good enough. He harassed me relentlessly about that. I tried to defend myself, before knowing better, and he seemed to enjoy that immensely. He then used that situation against me on my progress report as being delinquent in meeting deadlines. I was furious.

Out of exhaustion and disillusionment, I cried out to God about this man. I told God that I felt that I had become this man's target and asked Him to remove me from this situation. God told me to submit to his authority. I couldn't believe it. God said stop fighting, acquiesce and do what he is asking, without questions or feedback. I thought it would be hard, but when God tells you to do something, He also gives you plenty of grace to do it. So I did what God said.

Before I knew it, the manager began to soften and allowed

me to perform at my best because he was no longer actively hunting me. I turned in work products that forced him to give me kudos. Occasionally, he tried to poke me or get me off guard, but I didn't take the bait. In fact, I taught others the best way to deal with him was like quicksand; the less you struggle or oppose him, the better things will be for you. Finally, when a new job opportunity within the company became available, that same tormenting manager gave me a very nice recommendation.

God always know better than us. That manager did eventually get his divine retribution for all he did to me and others. Let's just say God gave it to him in the 'end'.

Chapter 6

"The LORD, the Lord, the compassionate and gracious God, slow to anger, abounding in Love and faithfulness, maintaining love to thousands, and forgiving wickedness, rebellion and sin. Yet he does not leave the guilty unpunished; he punishes the children and their children for the sin of the parents to the third and fourth generation."

Exodus 34:6–7, (NIV)

Especially Wicked bullies are people that have no shred of compassion, empathy or kindness towards others that they feel are in their way. Out of an inordinate and irrational notion of self-entitlement, these people operate as juggernauts who destroy, obliterate, massacre and eliminate anything and everything that deters them from what they feel is their divine right to have. Add authority and power to these especially wicked people and you have a recipe for sheer and utter disaster for anyone in their realm of control. It's equivalent to leaving a rabid dog in the house with babies. The potential for carnage is inevitable. Thankfully, such a person will not last for long. Yes, for a time these types of people will be in the world, and will inflict atrocities and wickedness unopposed. "The [spiritually ignorant] fool has said in his heart, 'There is no God'. They are corrupt, they have committed repulsive and unspeakable deeds; There is no one who does good" (Psalm 14:1, AMP).

As believers, we are not powerless against those who are powerful and wicked. Do like our aforesaid victors did; CRY OUT TO GOD against those war-mongering leaders, racist hate-spreaders, dictators, warlords, barbarians, sexual predators, kidnappers, oppressors, fowlers, and tormentors. God sees them and knows of their wicked deeds. And just like the Nephilim, He will WIPE THEM OUT.

KING HEROD THE GREAT: Especially Wicked Bully

The Gospels of Matthew and Luke tell us the story of Christ's birth. These books, albeit very briefly, mention King Herod of Judea who was the ruler at the time. Simply reading these two books of the Bible does not provide an abundance of detail about the level of wickedness that King Herod displayed toward his own people during the early years of Christ's life in the world. Some facts and tidbits of information were disclosed but many were not, for whatever reason. Unknown as to why the Bible did not go into detail regarding King Herod left me very curious. From my study of God's word, I have found three crucial patterns, of many, that were personal revelation to me, when it comes to understanding God. (1) He is love, (2) He is forgiving, and (3) He will avenge.

God will cut down like chaff and throw into a roaring fire those who are habitually and especially wicked. Malachi 4:1-3 (NASB) reads; "For behold, the day is coming, burning like a furnace; and all the arrogant and every evildoer will be chaff; and the day that is coming will set them ablaze, says the Lord of hosts, 'so that it will leave them neither root nor branch.' 'But for you who fear My name, the sun of righteousness will rise with healing in its wings; and you will go forth and skip about like calves from the stall. You will tread down the wicked, for they will be ashes under the soles of your feet on the day which I am preparing,' says the Lord of hosts." So when I read in the Bible that King Herod ordered the mass killing of all babies two years and under, I was quickly reminded of all the other bullies discussed thus far, and especially pharaoh. Pharaoh also made it lawful for the people to kill all Jewish baby boys by throwing them into the Nile. It was never mentioned if any Egyptians took part in the pharaoh's death mission, but we know the midwives most certainly did not obey what pharaoh asked them to do. However, King Herod went the extra step and ordered his soldiers to carry out his wicked commands. Matthew 2:16 (AMP) says, "Then Herod, when he realized that he had been tricked by the magi, was extremely angry, and he sent [soldiers] and put to death all the male children in Bethlehem and in all that area who were two years old and under, according to the date which he had learned from the magi." Then, only three verses later in Matthew 2:19 (AMP), we read "But when Herod died, an angel of the Lord appeared in a dream to Joseph in Egypt, and said, 'Get up! Take the Child and his mother, and go to the land of Israel; for those who sought the child's life are dead.' Then Joseph got up, and took the Child and His mother, and came into the land of Israel." This was too brief for me and I needed to know and understand exactly what happened. In Matthew 2:13 Joseph is warned by an angel to leave Bethlehem and go to Egypt to escape from Herod the madman. For a period of time Joseph and the family are in Egypt, but nothing else is mentioned regarding Herod until that intriguing morsel of information in Matthew 2:19. What happened to Herod!? How did he die and what were the circumstances? Knowing how God will SHOW UP and SHOW OUT when it comes to His people, and because Jesus was His only **begotten** son, I knew something dramatic and divinely orchestrated had to have happened to Herod. I am so glad I investigated further because this story is one that could not and should not be omitted from a book about overcoming bullies. It must be told.

Because our Holy Bible did not expound on all that King Herod did, I turned to outside sources that would help to not only shed light on all that King Herod did, but to also bring to light why the Bible possibly did not reveal those things. My thoughts as to why things were not revealed will be discussed after I present what was discovered regarding King Herod. King Herod's existence was confirmed in an article titled *Herod* written by contributing author Stewart Henry Perowne and published online on June 28, 2016 in the Encyclopedia Britannica. Herod was born in 73 BCE and —died March/April, 4 BCE. He was the Roman-appointed king of Judaea (37–4 BCE) (Perowne, 2016). BCE (Before Common Era) and BC (Before Christ) mean the same thing. At the age of 32, Herod was appointed ruler or tetrarch of Galilee by Mark Antony, the Roman general under Julius Caesar. Herod was favored by Rome and was promoted to the supreme Ruler of Judea at the age of 36.

Prior to Rome declaring Herod as supreme ruler, Judea was under the rule of the Hasmonean (Has-mō-ne-an) empire; a longstanding Jewish dynasty. But like most dynasties, infighting between the heirs brought about its demise. Two Hasmonean brothers: Hyrcanus (Hire-can-us) and Aristobulus (Aris-stah-bū-lus) were in a contentious struggle for power over the empire after the death of their father Alexander Jannaeus (Jan-nee-us) and their mother Alexandra Salome (sol-a-may). After Alexander passed, Salome ruled and appointed the older son Hyrcanus to be the High Priest over Judea. When she passed, she again named Hyrcanus to be king in her place. However, after only three months on the throne, the younger brother Aristobulus tried to oust Hyrcanus in a dramatic coup. It was during these times of instability and civil unrest that Herod and his father, Antipater (An-TIP-puh-ter), were weaving political alliances with the Rome. Because the Hasmonean's were battling back and forth, "the senate there [in Rome] nominated him [Herod] king of Judaea and equipped him with an army to make good his claim. In the year 37 BCE, at the age of 36, Herod became the unchallenged ruler of Judaea, a position he was to maintain for 32 years" (Perowne, 2016).

According to Perowne,

> Herod endowed his realm with massive fortresses and splendid cities, of which the two greatest were new, and largely pagan, foundations: the port of Caesarea Palaestinae on the coast between Joppa (Jaffa) and Haifa, which was afterward to become the capital of Roman Palestine; and Sebaste on the long-desolate site of ancient Samaria. At Herodium in the Judaean desert Herod built a great palace, which archaeologists in 2007 tentatively identified as the site of his tomb. In Jerusalem he built the fortress of Antonia, portions of which may still be seen beneath the convents on the Via Dolorosa

[believed to be the path that Jesus walked on the way to his crucifixion], and a magnificent palace (of which part survives in the citadel). His most grandiose creation was the Temple, which he wholly rebuilt.

Additional expository sources of information used to unearth the life and activities of King Herod was the translated book *Antiquities of the Jews* written by controversial, yet renowned Jewish historian Flavius Josephus and lastly, an article titled *What Disease Killed King Herod?* found online at the National Geographic website. Josephus was considered controversial because, although he was a Jew, he was seen as an opportunistic traitor of the Jewish people when it concerned Rome. Sentiments from contemporary Jewish scholars and historians, as well as Jews of his time period, toward Josephus was similar to Herod in that Josephus was "Rome's puppet." Josephus, however did not have the power, authority or army as King Herod. Therefore, Josephus' attempt to memorialize the history of Jews, according to him, was neither to paint the Jews nor the Romans in any particular light, but only to present the facts. Josephus, in his own words, tells his motivations for writing *Antiquities of the Jews* as translated by William Whiston:

> Those who undertake to write histories, do not, I perceive, take that trouble on one and the same account, but for many reasons, and those such as are very different one from another. For some of them apply themselves to this part of learning to show their skill in composition, and that they may therein acquire a reputation for speaking finely: others of them there are, who write histories in order to gratify those that happen to be concerned in them, and on that account have spared no pains, but rather gone beyond their own abilities in the performance: but others there are, who, of necessity and by force, are driven to write history, because they are concerned in the facts, and so cannot excuse themselves from committing them to writing, for the advantage of posterity; nay, there are not a few who are induced to draw their historical facts out of darkness into light, and to produce them for the benefit of the public, on account of the great importance of the facts themselves

with which they have been concerned. Now of these several reasons for writing history, I must profess the two last were my own… (*Josephus, 1preface1*).

As a recap before we unveil all that was gleaned regarding Herod, Matthew 2:16 told us that King Herod was furious that the baby Messiah and His family had evaded his capture, and so he ordered his army to kill all the boys in Bethlehem and its vicinity who were two years old and under. Referring again to what Perowne revealed, Herod divorced his first wife Doris and sent her and his child away. His motivation was to marry Princess Mariamne (mary-am-nee) and form a political/military alliance with the powerful yet beleaguered, Hasmonean empire. To Herod's credit, it does attest that he was deeply in love with Mariamne. But due to his wicked and suspicious mind he killed Mariamne, "her two sons, her brother, her grandfather, and her mother" (*Perowne, 2016*).

At the end of Herod's life, instead of putting aside his

wickedness, he amplified it. Not only did he order the execution of the innocents, Herod also asked his (remaining) family members to make a deathbed oath to him by agreeing to massacre all the noble men in the Jewish community once he died. This would make it appear that the Jews were mourning him when the family, subsequently and deceptively announced that he too had died. In effect Herod was continuing to conspire wickedness despite his ever-failing health by orchestrating a sinister con to dupe the Jews into mourning him because he was afraid that no one in the Jewish community would mourn him because the Jews detested him. Josephus wrote the following concerning his wicked request:

> So he deplored his condition, with tears in his eyes, and obtested them by the kindness due from them, as of his kindred, and by the faith they owed to God, and begged of them that they would not hinder him of this honorable mourning at his funeral. So they promised him not to transgress his commands (*Josephus, 17.6.5*).

To translate the above; with tears in his eyes, the dying Herod humbly begged his family, for what he felt he was due and what they owed him; not to hinder his final request, but because of their faith in God to carry out his wicked entreaty for him to have an honorable mourning at his funeral.

Furthermore, Josephus sums up Herod's deplorable actions with the following which requires no further translation by me:

> Now any one may easily discover the temper of this man's mind, which not only took pleasure in doing what he had done formerly against his relations, out of the love of life, but by those commands of his which savored of no humanity; since he took care, when he was departing out of this life, that the whole nation should be put into mourning, and indeed made desolate of their dearest kindred, when he gave order that one out of every family should be slain, although they had done nothing that was unjust, or that was against him, nor were they accused of any other crimes; while it is usual for those who have any regard to virtue to lay aside their hatred at such a time, even with respect to those they justly

esteemed their enemies (*Josephus, 17.6.6*).

To tie in all the evidence of Herod's wicked activities, the National Geographic article employs more of Josephus' narratives and provides this additional background on King Herod; "Some of his actions were much less glorious: He executed one of his 10 wives and three of his 14 children, and might have ordered the infamous Slaughter of the Innocents in his quest to kill the baby Jesus" (Trivedi). Lastly, Josephus eloquently defines the person that was Herod with this epitaph: "A man he was of great barbarity towards all men equally, and a slave to his passion; but above the consideration of what was right" (*Josephus, 17.8.1*).

So now that we have firmly established that King Herod was a monster of the worst kind who killed with ease, it's time to find out how he met his final end. Josephus, whether you like him or not, does a wonderful job of giving us the rich, image inspiring details of Herod's final days. Josephus wrote that Herod, had a severe distemper (disease or infection), as a punishment by

God for his sins. He had fever inside his body which caused him to lose his appetite and also caused internal pain. His entrails (intestinal organs) were very sore full of ulcers (pus-filled lesions and necrosis (death) of the tissue) and the most excruciating of his pain was in his colon where a transparent liquid had settled itself about his feet and at the bottom of his belly. Additionally, his male sexual organ was putrefied (decomposing and foul-smelling) and produced worms. He had difficulty breathing and his breath was abhorrent with a violent stench. Written in Josephus' own words:

> But now Herod's distemper greatly increased upon him after a severe manner, and this by God's judgment upon him for his sins; for a fire glowed in him slowly, which did not so much appear to the touch outwardly, as it augmented his pains inwardly; for it brought upon him a vehement appetite to eating, which he could not avoid to supply with one sort of food or other. His entrails were also ex-ulcerated, and the chief violence of his pain lay on his colon; an aqueous and transparent liquor also had settled itself about his feet, and a like matter afflicted him at

the bottom of his belly. Nay, further, his privy-
member was putrefied, and produced worms;
and when he sat upright, he had a difficulty of
breathing, which was very loathsome, on
account of the stench of his breath (*Josephus,
17.6.5*).

According to Trivedi in his National Geographic article,
a physician by the name of Dr. Jan Hirschmann at the
University of Washington School of Medicine in Seattle
was able to narrow down what Herod's disease was
using the account provided by Josephus regarding
King Herod's symptoms. Dr. Hirschmann thinks the king
probably died of chronic kidney disease, complicated
by a particularly nasty case of gangrene, called
Fournier's gangrene. The National Organization of Rare
Disorders or NORD defines Fournier's gangrene as "an
acute necrotic infection of the scrotum; penis; or
perineum (pair-a-ne-um). It is characterized by scrotum
pain and redness with rapid progression to gangrene
and sloughing of tissue. Fournier's gangrene is usually
secondary to perirectal [tissues surrounding the rectum]
or periurethral [tissues surrounding the urethra]
infections associated with local trauma, operative
procedures, or urinary tract disease" (*Bracho-Riquelme,*

2017). Trivedi also stated that Dr. Hirschmann focused his medical investigation of Herod on Josephus' account that Herod suffered from insatiable itching. From that symptom, the doctor narrowed the possibility of diseases down to less than ten. From there, Dr. Hirschmann then included the information regarding Herod's genital ailments according to Trivedi. This symptom actually stumped him, but Dr. Hirschmann ultimately concluded that Herod's string of symptoms more closely resembled chronic kidney failure with an acute case of genital gangrene, (caused by a rare infection) A.K.A. Fournier's gangrene.

I believe the reason that King Herod's extensive wickedness as well as how he was ultimately struck down with all his grisly infirmities was not revealed in the Bible was to spare those who may be easily disturbed by the gruesome specifics. The same way we don't provide grotesque details or worse yet, reprehensibly take pleasure in those who have suffered, or were killed in horrendous tragedies such as accidents whether man made or divinely established. As people, we must protect our body mind and spirit from soul shocking, excessively violent, gruesome and grotesque things which can lead to a desensitization to the afflictions of others. Else, we would be no less atrocious than the person that was denounced by God as evil. Perhaps God, being so kind and benevolent toward His people, wanted to spare us the horrific details regarding Herod for our own salvation and benefit. But, there is nothing wrong with studying to edify and to know God. In fact, God wants us to know His word and go deeper. When you stick with God, nothing will be able to deceive you, bully you, scare you, or harm you. Trust in Him and stick with Him in everything.

The Hasmonean Dynasty Diagram

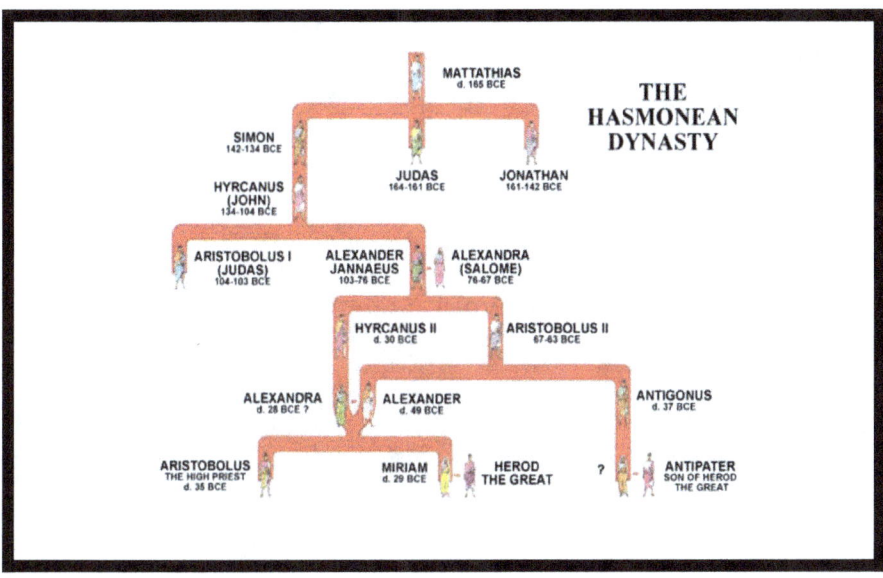

(GOOGLE)

King Herod's Family Tree Diagram

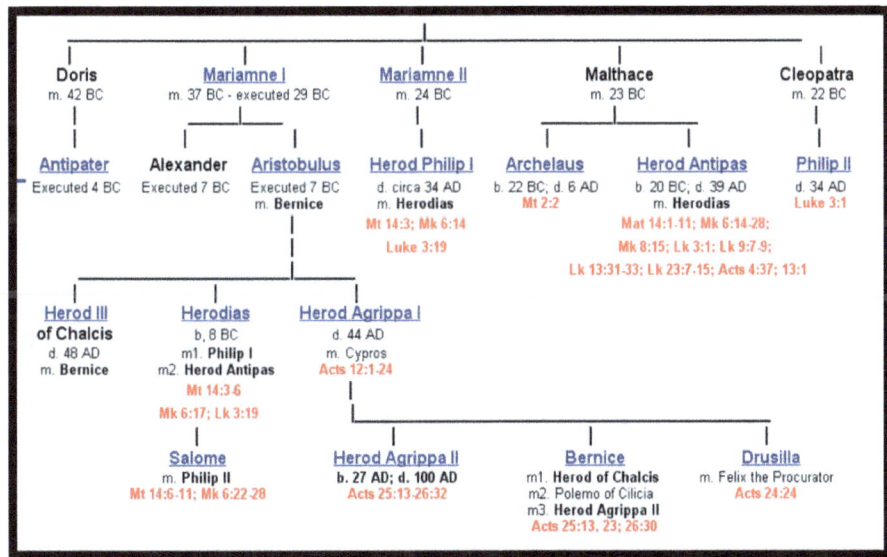

(GOOGLE)

Chapter 7

"The high priest stood up before them and asked Jesus, 'Are you not going to answer? What is this testimony that these men are bringing against you?' But Jesus remained silent and gave no answer."

Mark 14:61, NIV

JESUS CHRIST Our Perfect Example of Victory Over Bullies

For anyone who has ever been or is currently mentally or physically confined, sick, abused, tormented, cast down by life, society or anything; Jesus Christ, our Lord and Savior, is our ultimate Healer, Counselor, Consoler and Redeemer. You must trust, rely, and lean on Him to be your guiding light in this dark evil world. He has already released you from your bully tormentors when He died for all of us. Jesus understood that His suffering was for God's divine purpose, to pay in full our sin debt forever. Romans 6:23 (NIV) says, "But now that you have been set free from sin and have become slaves to God, the fruit you reap leads to holiness, and the outcome is eternal life. For the wages of sin is death, but the gift of God is eternal life in Christ Jesus our Lord."

Since He paid the ultimate price, we are now fully redeemed and never have to return to a state of captivity to anyone or anything except for God who loves us and wants the best for us. But if we do not know this, we will continue to find ourselves held captive by life's trials and tribulations, and by opportunistic bullies who will incessantly try to knock naïve targets around who don't know that Christ has already opened their prison doors so they can walk out and not continue to allow themselves to stay enslaved, afraid and debilitated in fear. "They arrested the apostles and put them in a public jail. But during the night an angel of the Lord opened the prison doors, and leading them out, he said, 'Go, stand and continue to tell the people in the temple [courtyards] the whole message of this Life [the eternal life revealed by Christ and found through faith in Him]'" (Acts 5:18-20, AMP). Know that you are free.

Thankfully, Peter reminds us that Jesus is our example of how to deal with tormenting bullies: "For [as a believer] you have been called for this purpose, since Christ suffered for you, leaving you an example, so that you may follow in His footsteps" (1 Peter 2:21, AMP). Even while Jesus was going through unimaginable suffering He trusted, relied and lean on God in the midst of the abuse because Jesus knew that the Father was in control of his life, not these evil bullies. Jesus also knew that he would eventually be killed, and in Matthew

20:19 foretold of his death when He said, "They will condemn him to death and will hand him over to the Gentiles to be mocked and flogged and crucified. On the third day he will be raised to life!" The second part of that verse tells you that Jesus overcame his tormentors in an awesome, fantastic, and death-defying fashion. He proved to those who try to kill your body, mind and soul that when you are with God, are in God, and are of God, nothing will ever destroy you, not anything. Here are great examples of how to "*do what Jesus did*" when you are plagued by bullies:

- **Continue to speak truth and life** to those who *do* love and care for you. In Mark 3:22 (NIV) Jesus was lied upon; "He is possessed by Beelzebub! By the prince of demons, he is driving out demons." Jesus was exorcising demons from people who were possessed, and for this reason he was stupidly accused of being the devil. This makes no sense whatsoever, and Jesus precisely dissected their contradictory accusations when he asked his disciples, "How can Satan drive out Satan?" And you know what? He made perfect sense. If you're evil, you wouldn't drive out evil, you would revel in it. But notice that Jesus did not ask this question of his accusers. He knew that they would not accept any sound reasoning because they had already made their mind up to hate and despise him and therefore conspired to destroy him. Save your breath against your tormentor. Don't try to reason or justify your good qualities to a bully. A bully does not operate within reason; they do not willingly yield or relent of their wicked behavior. Just like the Nephilim, Saul, Amnon, Nabal, Pharaoh, Rehoboam, Haman, Sanballat and Tobiah, Peninnah, Jezebel, Athaliah, and any other bully. The situation always requires God's divine intervention to remove a bully in order for them to stop. Jesus understood this and knew that it would not help in any way for him to try and justify himself to these monstrous, tormenting bullies.

- **Call upon your heavenly Father**. Jesus cried out to God. While Jesus was detained by the Sadducees and Pharisees, "They stripped him and put a scarlet robe on him, and then twisted together a crown of thorns and set it on his head. They put a staff in his right hand. Then they knelt in front of him and mocked him. 'Hail, king of the Jews!', they said. They spit on him, and took the staff and struck him on the head again and again. After they had mocked him, they took off the robe and put his own clothes on him. Then they led him away to crucify him" (Matthew 27:28-31, NIV). Before Jesus was taken away by them, he had been fervently praying to God. In Luke 22:42 (NIV) Jesus prays the following; "Father, if you are willing, take this cup from me; yet not my will, but yours be done." The very next verse reveals just how Jesus was able to withstand all that he endured: "An angel from heaven appeared to him and strengthened him" (Luke 22:43, NIV). God will give you strength to endure all your trials when you call on Him. He may not deliver you in the manner in which you imagined, but God will sustain you. Trust, rely and lean on God in prayer. Although Jesus died on the cross as a result of the torture he endured at the hands of his tormentors, God surely delivered Him. When you cry out to God in prayer, He does hear you and will deliver you.

- **Speak no ill about your tormentors**. Jesus opened not his mouth in retaliation. "While being reviled and insulted, He did not revile or insult in return; while suffering, He made no threats [of vengeance], but kept trusting Himself to Him who judges fairly" (1 Peter 2:23, AMP). He understood that words have power, and the power of life and death are in the tongue (Proverbs 18:21) and the tongue can ensnare those who are not careful with their words. In John 14:30 (AMP) Jesus explains; "I will not speak with you much longer, for the ruler of the world (Satan) is coming. And he has no claim on Me [no power over Me nor anything that he can use against Me]." His tormentors had already tried and convicted Jesus without due process, so there was no point in him trying to argue, justify or defend himself. He was solely trusting, relying and leaning on God.

- **Accept the fact that they hate you or intensely dislike you** for whatever reason. Jesus was hated and accepted this fact without trying to explain himself or beg for their friendship. In John 15:18-22

(MSG) it reads, "If you find the godless world is hating you, remember it got its start hating me. If you lived on the world's terms, the world would love you as one of its own. But since I picked you to live on God's terms and no longer on the world's terms, the world is going to hate you. When that happens, remember this: Servants don't get better treatment than their masters. If they beat on me, they will certainly beat on you. If they did what I told them, they will do what you tell them. They are going to do all these things to you because of the way they treated me, because they don't know the One who sent me. If I hadn't come and told them all this in plain language, it wouldn't be so bad. As it is, they have no excuse. Hate me, hate my Father---It's all the same..." Jesus never cared to try and convince his haters.

- **Forgive those who persecute you** even while you are being persecuted. This is very difficult but necessary so that you will quickly go through those hard times unscathed. Our attitude during trouble times will determine how we get through our troubles. In Luke 23:34 (NIV), while nailed to the cross Jesus said, "Father, forgive them, for they do not know what they are doing." Jesus forgave very quickly and as a result He was speedily delivered by God while on that cross. His captors were already planning to break both of his legs to expedite his death, but when they were about to break Jesus' legs, they discovered that he had already expired: "The soldiers therefore came and broke the legs of the first man who had been crucified with Jesus, and then those of the other. But when they came to Jesus and found that he was already dead, they did not break his legs" (John 19:32-34, NIV). In Acts 7:59, Stephen a servant of Jesus, was preaching the good news of Jesus Christ after Jesus was crucified. The unbelieving people accused him of blasphemy at all that he spoke regarding Jesus, so they dragged him outside of the city and started stoning Stephen. Then Stephen quickly forgives them in Acts 7:60 (AMP): "Then falling on his knees [in worship], he cried out loudly, 'Lord, do not hold this sin against them [do not charge them]!' When he said this, he fell asleep [in death]." God did not let Jesus or

Stephen linger in their suffering. Forgiveness is the shortest and most direct route to overcoming the injurious effects of your enemies. Do it instantly so that you do not suffer a second longer.

- **Overcome and walk out your victory!** Jesus overcame! In John 16:33 (NIV) Jesus said to his disciples, "I have told you these things, so that in me you may have peace. In this world you will have trouble. But take heart! I have overcome the world." And in Luke 10:19 (NIV) He said, "I have given you the authority to trample on snakes and scorpions and to overcome all the power of the enemy; nothing will harm you." Though Jesus went to be with the Father, he also returned again in three days to fulfill the divine prophecy. "He went once for all into the Holy Place [the Holy of Holies of heaven, into the presence of God], and not through the blood of goats and calves, but through His own blood, having obtained and secured eternal redemption [that is, the salvation of all who personally believe in Him as Savior]" (Hebrews 9:12, AMP). If death could not contain Jesus then "stop weeping; behold, the Lion that is from the tribe of Judah, the Root of David, has overcome... (Revelation 5:5, NASB). Know that our Father in heaven can and will deliver you from your tormentors, once and for all.

EPILOGUE

"We gave you strict orders not to teach in this name, 'Yet you have filled Jerusalem with your teaching and are determined to make us guilty of this man's blood'"

Acts 5:28, NIV

From Saul to Paul: Pursuing Persecutor to Championing Cheerleader

After Jesus was crucified, his followers were empowered with the Holy Spirit that descended on them like tongues of fire. They began to do all kinds of acts of healing, speaking in foreign tongues and other wondrous acts and miracles. The believers unified and formed a true church with the singular mission of spreading the good news of Jesus Christ the Messiah to all of the world. Out of jealousy, the Pharisees and Sadducees treated the believers very harshly. The apostles were so filled with power, they were healing people, opening blind eyes; physically and figuratively, and setting people free from all kinds of ailments, bondages and suffering.

The apostles were also letting people know of the freedom in Jesus Christ. When Jesus was alive He often spoke of the hypocrisy of the Jewish leaders. In Matthew 23:4 (MSG) Jesus said, "Instead of giving you God's Law as food and drink by which you can banquet on God, they package it in bundles of rules, loading you down like pack animals. They seem to take pleasure in watching you stagger under these loads and wouldn't think of lifting a finger to help. Their lives are perpetual fashion shows, embroidered prayer shawls one day and flowery prayers the next. They love to sit at the head table at church dinners, basking in the most prominent positions, preening in the radiance of public flattery, receiving honorary degrees, and getting called 'Doctor' and 'Reverend.'"

The apostles also openly testified about Jesus' resurrection. The Sadducees did not believe in the resurrection and were very critical of those who spoke of resurrections. "They were greatly disturbed because the apostles were teaching the people, proclaiming in Jesus the resurrection of the dead" (Acts 4:2, NIV). The Sadducees also opposed the Pharisees because they believed in resurrection. The Sadducees were filled with jealousy and arrested the apostles and put them in jail but they were supernaturally freed from their captors by an angel of the Lord in the middle of the night. That still did not stop the Jewish leaders from coming after them. The Sanhedrin elders who judged the citizens of

Israel demanded the apostles to not teach in Jesus' name. But Peter and the other apostles boldly told them, "We must obey God rather than human beings!" (Acts 5:29).

The Sanhedrin also arranged and sanctioned the beating of the apostles for preaching in the name of Jesus, but the apostles rejoiced in their suffering for Christ the Messiah. They were called blasphemers for boldly proclaiming all that Christ had done and how He was the word made flesh and how He was with God from the beginning. Because the apostles were relentlessly oppressed, Stephen, "a man full of faith and of the Holy Spirit (Acts 6:5, NIV)" was violently dragged outside of the city gates and stoned to death. "And Saul approved of their killing him" (Acts 8:1, NIV).

Saul of Tarsus was a staunch persecutor, and hunter of the apostles of the Way. Saul was zealous for his religious beliefs to the point of working with the Sanhedrin. In Philippians 3:5-6, Paul states; "Circumcised when I was eight days old, of the nation of Israel, of the tribe of Benjamin, a Hebrew of Hebrews [an exemplary Hebrew]; as to the [observance of the] Law, a Pharisee, as to my zeal [for Jewish tradition], a persecutor of the church; and as to the righteousness [supposed right living] which [my fellow Jews believe] is the Law, I proved myself blameless." And in Acts 22:4 while speaking in Aramaic, the native tongue of the Jews, Saul also said, "I persecuted the followers of this Way to their death, arresting both men and women and throwing them into prison, as the high priest and all the Council can themselves testify. I even obtained letters from them to their associates in Damascus, and went there to bring these people as prisoners to Jerusalem to be punished."

After witnessing Stephen getting stoned, it says that Saul approved of their killing him, and he went to the high priest "and he asked for letters [of authority] from him to the synagogues at Damascus, so that if he found any men or women there belonging to the Way [believers, followers of Jesus the Messiah], men and women alike, he could arrest them and bring them bound [with chains] to Jerusalem" (Acts 9:2, AMP). As he was nearing Damascus on his mission to wrangle up the believers, "suddenly a light from heaven flashed around him and Saul fell to the ground and heard a voice say to him, 'Saul, Saul, why do you persecute me?' (Acts 9:3-4, NIV). Jesus sternly said, "I am Jesus, whom you are persecuting, Now get up and go in the city and you will be told what you must do'" (Acts 9:5-6, NIV).

Saul was so convicted of the error of his ways for persecuting the believers with his unrighteous anger toward Jesus and the believers, he was deeply mortified and remorseful for his actions. And because Paul humbled himself before Christ and took up the cross of Jesus to loudly proclaim that Jesus was the Messiah, he was given a very special and befitting assignment: "Be brave; for as you have solemnly and faithfully witnessed about Me at Jerusalem, so you must also testify at Rome" (Acts 23:11, AMP). Paul's new mission was to preach the Way of Jesus to all the non-Jewish people called the Gentiles. So Saul, became well renowned by his Roman (Latin) name, Paul. Paul's teachings and letters to the various people can be found in the following books of the Bible: Romans, 1st and 2nd Corinthians, Galatians, Ephesians, Philippians,

Colossians, 1st and 2nd Thessalonians, 1st and 2nd Timothy, Titus, and Philemon. He became one of many of Jesus' loudest cheerleaders by broadcasting all that happened to him on the road to Damascus, to the Jews and Gentiles. Paul's witness was so powerful, that he converted many people to the Way of Jesus Christ and died a martyr's death in the name of Jesus.

This tells me that even our tormentors will eventually bow down to our Lord and Savior. Whether by choice or force. Paul humbly and obediently received God's rebuke and therefore His redemption. Perhaps while dying, when Stephen prayed and asked God to forgive his persecutors, was the turning point as to why God chose Paul on that road to Damascus and ultimately and graciously pardoned and gave him a second chance. What a great lesson we have here; We need to pray for our enemies so that God can begin to deal with them and perhaps God will turn our persecutors into our cheerleaders. If not, we now know how to fight and be victorious none the less. What a win/win for all of God's people.

THE END

References

Bracho-Riquelme, R. L. (2017). *Fournier Gangrene.* Retrieved April 16, 2017, from National Organization for Rare Disorders: https://rarediseases.org/rare-diseases/fournier-gangrene

Encarta World Dictionary. (n.d.). *Microsoft's Digital Encyclopedia.* Retrieved 2017

Google. (n.d.). Retrieved April 21, 2017, from Google Images: https://goo.gl/images/rropbf

Google. (n.d.). Retrieved April 21, 2017, from Crandall University: https://goo.gl/images/9yU47C

Josephus, F., Whiston, W., & Auburn and Buffalo, &. B. (1895). *Perseus Digital Library Project.* Retrieved April 16, 2016, from Tufts University: http://www.perseus.tufts.edu/hopper/text?doc=urn:cts:greekLit:tlg0526.tlg001.perseus-eng1:17.6.5

MSN Encarta. (1981-2015). Retrieved April 22, 2017, from Computer Desktop Encyclopedia: http://encyclopedia2.thefreedictionary.com/MSN+Encarta

Perowne, S. H. (2016, June 28). *Herod.* Retrieved April 16, 2017, from Encyclopædia Britannica: https://www.britannica.com/biography/Herod-king-of-Judaea

Strong, J. (unknown). *Strongs Exhaustive Concordance.* Peabody, MA: Henrickson Publishers.

Trivedi, B. (2002, January 28). *National Geographic.* Retrieved April 16, 2017, from National Geographic Society : http://news.nationalgeographic.com/news/2002/01/0128_020128_King Herod.html

ABOUT THE AUTHOR

Darnnell Reese is a bully's worst nightmare—and a survivor's greatest ally. A U.S. Army veteran and former Military Intelligence Analyst, she served in Operation Desert Storm during the Gulf War and faced life-threatening situations both on and off the battlefield. Those early trials, along with later battles involving illness, workplace hostility, and profound personal challenges, became the giants she learned to slay through God's power alone.

Every hardship pushed her deeper into Scripture, where she discovered unwavering strength, spiritual clarity, and the authority to fight back—God's way. Today, Darnnell is an advocate, intercessor, and powerful voice for those navigating fear, injustice, and spiritual warfare. Her mission is simple: to help others activate victory in their own lives, no matter the size of the giant.

Darnnell is the author of multiple faith-based works, including *Victorious! Defeating Bullies & Giants God's Way*, *In All Seriousness... Totally Funny Bible Stories*, and her critically acclaimed memoir *Blanket Party in Desert Storm*, which received a **Kirkus Reviews "GET IT" recommendation** and a **January 15 Kirkus Indie Spotlight** selection.

She lives in Fort Washington, Maryland with her loving husband, Terrence. Their daughter, Deidra—an accomplished fashion designer—remains one of their greatest joys.

If Darnnell's work has blessed you, she would love to hear from you. Visit her author website at reeseauthor.com for book news, reviews, and ways to connect. A review on Amazon or Goodreads goes a long way — your encouragement truly blesses the author in return.

www.ingramcontent.com/pod-product-compliance
Lightning Source LLC
Chambersburg PA
CBHW070914130626
46555CB00001B/129